The Hemlock Spruce.

FOREST TREES,

FOR

SHELTER, ORNAMENT and PROFIT.

A

PRACTICAL MANUAL

FOR

THEIR CULTURE AND PROPAGATION.

BY ARTHUR BRYANT, SR.

ILLUSTRATED.

NEW YORK:
HENRY T. WILLIAMS, PUBLISHER.
OFFICE OF THE HORTICULTURIST.
1871.

VAN BENTHUYSEN PRINTING HOUSE,
Stereotypers and Printers,
Albany, N. Y.

PREFACE.

The present work was undertaken at the solicitation of some friends of the author, who felt the need of a more thorough and practical compend upon Forest Culture than any now before the public. The writer has from boyhood interested himself in the planting of trees, and while he cannot boast of very extensive operations in their culture, he hopes that the results of his own observation and experience, combined with what he has been able to collect from other sources, may constitute a work acceptable to those interested in the subject.

Forest culture in America is yet in its infancy. The energies of our rural population have hitherto been largely employed in the extermination of the woods; and it is but recently that the necessity of their partial reproduction has attracted any considerable attention. Time and experience, particularly in the prairie regions, will doubtless develop new facts in regard to the adaptation of the more valuable kinds of timber to the different soils. Species now little known may hereafter be extensively cultivated.

This work is designed for the northern portion of the United States, extending westward to the Rocky Mountains and southward to include Virginia, Kentucky, Missouri and Kansas. The vast treeless plains of the West, offer an almost limitless field for forest planting, and the States of Kansas and Nebraska are already taking the lead in the enterprise.

All, or nearly all the trees native within the limits assigned to this work are noticed, together with a considerable number of foreign origin.

The author acknowledges his indebtedness to the works of G. P. Marsh, Gray, Loudon, Michaux, Meehan, Hoopes, and others, for much valuable information. The botanical descriptions have been mostly taken, with slight change, from the works of Gray and Loudon. Acknowledgments are also due for assistance in various ways from personal friends of the author.

While it has been thought best to adopt a scientific arrangement and description of the trees noticed, no pains have been spared to render the practical part as plain and thorough as possible. Although the leading object of the work is to describe and recommend the culture of valuable timber trees, their ornamental character has not been neglected, and many are noticed of little worth for any but ornamental purposes.

The author has long regarded the reproduction of the more valuable forest trees, by means of artificial plantations, as a matter of great national importance. Should this work in any degree aid in so desirable an object, he will feel that the labor bestowed upon it has not been thrown away.

CHAPTER I.

INTRODUCTION.

It is admitted that Trees are essential to civilization, and the fact is acknowledged that man cannot advance in improvement beyond the rudest form of pastoral life, without the use of timber. The question next arises, whether or not our countrymen will go on recklessly destroying an article of absolute necessity and immense daily consumption, without regard to a source of future supply? The rapid destruction of our forests within the past few years is really appalling. The State of New York, which, not many years since, exported great quantities of pine lumber, now obtains a supply for home consumption from abroad. The forests of Maine are said to be so completely stripped, that scarcely a pine tree of old growth is to be seen. At the present rate of consumption, the pine woods of the Northwestern States are likely to be exhausted in less than twenty-five years. It was estimated that the amount of lumber cut in 1869, in the States of Michigan, Wisconsin and Minnesota, was 3,311,372,255 feet. To obtain this quantity, 883,032 acres, or 1,380 square miles, were stripped of their trees. The destruction of hard-wood forests is likewise very rapid. There is a constantly increasing demand for valuable kinds of timber for the manufacture of machinery, farming implements, furniture, railway cars and wooden work of every description. Millions of ties, and millions of cords of firewood, are annually required by railroads. There can be no doubt that previous to the settlement of Central and Northern Illinois, the quantity of timber was annually diminished by the ravages of fire. When these ravages were in a measure stopped, a dense growth of young trees sprang up in the scattered woodlands, and twenty years since there was more wood than at the first settlement of the country. With the introduction of railroads commenced the destruction of the forests. It may safely be estimated that two-thirds of the full-grown timber in Northern Illinois has been destroyed within eighteen years past. Tracts of thriving young wood, whose annual growth added at least ten per cent to its value, have been cleared for firewood. The destruction still goes on. Such is the instability of our population, that woodlands which have been long preserved by their owners, sooner or later pass into the possession of those who, impatient to enjoy their value, and reckless of other considerations, ruthlessly fell them. Much of the land thus bared is of little value for any other purpose than the growth of wood, and is usually so closely pastured by domestic animals as effectually to prevent a new growth of trees.

In many of the older States the scarcity of timber is already severely felt. Hills and mountains which, not many years since, were crowned with wood, now rear their heads in unsightly baldness; and streams once affording permanent water power have become useless for that purpose, or unreliable for a great part of the year. It can hardly be supposed that, with our rapidly increasing population, the consumption of timber in future years will be greatly diminished, and the supply must ere long be brought from great distances at vastly increased expense. Much will doubtless be done by substituting brick, stone and iron for wood, and by the increased use of coal for fuel; but the demand for timber will always be immense. The necessity for providing for future supplies will soon be felt, and it is to be hoped that the interest which is beginning to manifest itself in some sections of our country will deepen to a general sense of the importance of the subject.

In Germany, France, and some other countries of Europe, the forests are the property of the government. Their management has been reduced to a system, and they are guarded with care from wanton depredation. Our own government, in times past, has had ample opportunity to reserve lands which, although valuable for their timber, were less desirable for settlement. Such tracts might, without great expense, be protected from devastation by agents employed for that purpose.* Something of the sort might still be done, but there is little hope of its accomplishment. Our National Legislature, in this respect at least, wholly destitute of statesmanlike forecast, panders to the rapacity of corporations, and hastens to squander the public domain. Most of our State legislators ignore the encouragement of tree planting altogether. Our Agricultural Societies, both State and county organizations, with few exceptions, liberally patronize the horse-jockey, while they wholly neglect the tree planter. The matter seems to depend almost entirely upon the enterprise and patriotism of individuals.

Let all, then, who have the opportunity to plant trees, awaken to a sense of the importance of the object. The evils attending a general destruction of

* Perhaps a better plan would be to transfer the woodlands to the individual States, whose authorities might be more efficient for their preservation than the U. S. Government. The latter could not—at least did not—protect the live oak woods of Florida, which were intended for the use of the navy. Timber growing on the public lands has everywhere been considered fair game for everybody, and Government is said in some instances to have paid high prices for timber stolen from its own woodlands. Nearly fifty years since, when the navigation of the secondary rivers of the West was of more importance than since the introduction of railroads, Dr. Drake, of Cincinnati, recommended the reservation by government of tracts of woodland around the head waters of the principal streams, as a means of preventing their diminution. Probably the doctor did not anticipate the time when these reserves might become important as a source of supplies of timber. It is scarcely necessary to say that his advice was disregarded.

the forests, if unchecked, will go on increasing with the lapse of years, until sections of our country become hopelessly sterile. The excuse that posterity has done nothing for us, is the plea of unmitigated selfishness. Americans owe more than any other nation to the toils, sacrifices and forethought of their forefathers, and it is our duty to transmit the inheritance we received from them to our descendants unimpaired by waste or neglect. The length of time required for the growth of timber from the seed to maturity shows conclusively that it was never designed in the order of nature for the exclusive use of a single generation.

CHAPTER II.

EVILS ATTENDING THE DESTRUCTION OF THE FORESTS.

G. P. Marsh, in his great work, entitled "Man and Nature," says: "There is good reason to believe that the surface of the habitable earth, in all the climates and regions which have been the abodes of dense and civilized populations, was, with few exceptions, already covered with a forest growth when it first became the home of man." Countries entirely covered with forests are fit only for the abode of savage races. As improvement advances the woods are partially felled, and the land fitted for the residence of a civilized people. But the arrangements of Nature cannot be entirely reversed with impunity. Either extreme produces the like effect—the total destruction of the forest unfits a country for the occupancy of any but a savage, or at best a nomadic population. The present condition of some of the countries around the Mediterranean Sea, once among the most productive in the world, and sustaining immense population, is graphically described in the following quotation from the above mentioned author:

"If we compare the present physical condition of the countries of which I am speaking (the Roman Empire), with the descriptions that ancient historians and geographers have given of their fertility and general capability of ministering to human uses, we shall find that more than one-half of their whole extent—including the provinces most celebrated for the profusion and variety of their spontaneous and their cultivated products, and for the wealth and social advancement of their inhabitants—is either deserted by civilized man and surrendered to hopeless desolation, or, at least, greatly reduced, both in productiveness and population. Vast forests have disappeared from mountain spurs and ridges; the vegetable earth accumulated beneath the trees by the decay of leaves and fallen trunks; the soil of the alpine pastures, which skirted and indented the woods, and the mould of the upland fields, are washed away; meadows once fertilized by irrigation are waste and unproductive, beeause the cisterns and reservoirs that supplied the ancient canals are broken, or the springs that fed them dried up; rivers, famous in history and song, have shrunk to humble brooklets; the willows that ornamented and protected the banks of the lesser water-courses are gone, and the rivulets have ceased to exist as perennial currents, because the little water that finds its way into their old channels is evaporated by the droughts of summer, or absorbed by the parched earth before it reaches the lowlands; the beds of the brooks have widened into broad expanses of sand and gravel, over which, though in the hot season passed dry shod, in winter sea-like torrents thunder; the entrances of navigable streams are obstructed by sand-bars; and harbors, once marts of an extensive commerce, are shoaled by the deposits of the rivers at whose mouths they lie."

The desolation of these countries is, undoubtedly, to be attributed mainly to the entire removal of the forests, although other causes have probably assisted in producing it. The forests of Mount Lebanon, once the source of supply for the neighboring countries, have long since disappeared; the mountain ranges of Syria, Cyrenaica, and the once populous and powerful kingdom of Persia, are now dry, barren ridges of naked rock, absolutely incapable of reproducing the woods which once covered them. Large tracts in the interior of Asia Minor, and even portions of Italy, are now a horrible desert, seamed with ravines and gullies, or piled with ridges of sand and gravel, and utterly irreclaimable to the use of man. Blanque, a French writer quoted by Marsh, speaking of the destruction of the forest in certain mountainous parts of France says, that he found not a living soul in districts where he had enjoyed hospitality thirty years before; the last inhabitants having been compelled to retreat when the last tree fell. Is there not great danger that, when the accumulating influence of causes now operating shall have had time to produce their full effect, portions of our own country may become alike uninhabitable? The level surface and geological formation of large tracts in the Mississippi valley will, doubtless, operate to mitigate or prevent such result; yet, when the slopes of the Rocky Mountains are stripped of their forests, and the sources of the Mississippi, and its tributaries, bared to the influence of sun and wind, who can say how great may be the evils arising from the diminution of the streams and the irregularities of the rainfall? The prospective scarcity and high price of timber, surely consequent upon the present devastation, is, of itself, a sufficient reason for planting forests; but when to this is superadded the probable ruin of habitable districts, and deterioration of climate in the whole country, the demand on patriotism is imperative for decisive and immediate action.

CHAPTER III.

FAVORABLE INFLUENCES OF THE FORESTS.

Among the advantages of a due proportion of woodland to that which is cleared, may be reckoned the diminution of the extremes of temperature. These extremes are greatest in countries destitute of wood. Land shaded by forests and covered with leaves, and snow undisturbed by winds, does not freeze to a great depth. The roots of trees penetrating to the unfrozen earth, act as conductors, and convey some portion of heat to the surrounding atmosphere. The advent of winds from colder regions is checked, and the stillness of the air renders the cold more endurable by man and beast; and, doubtless, equally so by vegetable life. The farmer, whose dwelling and outhouses are well sheltered by groves or screens, consumes less fuel in his house, and less forage in his stables and cattle yards, than he would if unprotected. In summer the soil of a wide expanse of open country becomes heated by the sun, and the temperature is higher and the winds hotter than in wooded regions. The sirocco and simoon, of the Asiatic and African deserts, are possible only in a country destitnte of trees. I have been informed by persons who have crossed the plains of our Southwestern territories, that they have been glad to seek shelter from the scorching wind on the lee-side of a wagon, even when that side was most exposed to the rays of the sun.

An important application of forest planting in Europe is the covering with trees, and rescuing from otherwise hopeless sterility, tracts of loose, shifting sand. One of the most extensive of these wastes is in the southwest part of France, on the shores of the Gulf of Gascony. The following description of this tract is from Loudon: "The downs there are composed of drifting sands covering 300 square miles. Bremontier compares the surface of this immense tract to a sea, which, when agitated to fury by a tempest, had been suddenly fixed and changed to sand. It offered nothing to the eye but a monotonous repetition of white wavy mountains perfectly destitute of vegetation. In times of violent storms of wind, the surface of these downs was entirely changed; what were hills of sand often becoming valleys, and the contrary. The sand on these occasions was often carried up into the interior of the country, covering cultivated fields, villages, and even entire forests. This takes place so gradually by the sand sweeping along the surface and thus raising it, or falling from the air in a shower of particles so fine as to be scarcely preceptible, that nothing is destroyed. The sand gradually rises among crops as if they were inundated with water, and the herbage and the tops of trees appear quite green and healthy, even to the moment of their being overwhelmed with the sand, which is so very fine as to resemble that used in England in hour glasses." This wide expanse of sand, rolling inland from the ocean, and threatening to bury the whole province, has been rendered stationary and harmless by planting it with the Maritime Pine (Pinus Pinaster). More than 100,000 acres have been planted; and great quantities of tar, resin, lamp-black, and timber of inferior quality are produced. In the north of Germany, tracts of loose drifting sand have, in like manner, been covered with forests of pine. The Ailanthus has been successfully employed in fixing the surface of sandy wastes in the south of Russia. In all these instances, lands previously not only worthless, but a positive nuisance, have been made to yield a profitable return.

CHAPTER IV.

INFLUENCE OF FORESTS UPON MOISTURE AND RAIN-FALL.

Except in cases of most excessive drought, the soil of a forest is always moist, and the trees of woodlands very rarely suffer from want of rain. The unfrozen earth becomes saturated by melted snow in Spring; the Summer rains are absorbed and retained by the loose soil carpeted with leaves, and the rapid evaporation of moisture is checked by shade.

Forests thus become reservoirs of humidity, lessening the dryness of the surrounding atmosphere, and aiding the perennial flow of springs and streams. Instances are on record of the drying up of springs and rivulets when the woods which shaded them were felled, and of their reappearance when the trees were suffered again to grow. The influence of woodlands in this respect must have been observed by every intelligent person who has bestowed any thought upon the subject.

2*

The effect of forests upon the total amount of rain-fall is a question upon which writers are not agreed, some denying their influence altogether. The increased amount of rain in Lower Egypt, since the formation of extensive plantations of trees by the rulers of that country, is often cited as a proof that the presence of forests increases the fall of rain. It is said that during the year 1869, there were fourteen rainy days at the Isthmus of Suez, where the rain had before been rarely, if ever, known. This was ascribed to the influence of recent forest plantations in the vicinity. Both theory and weight of evidence seem strongly to favor the position that more rain falls in wooded than in open countries. Be this as it may, it is certain that a more uniform degree of moisture in the atmosphere exists in and around forests than in cleared lands. Equally certain is it that, by promoting the frequency of showers, they equalize the distribution of the rain-fall through the different seasons, thus rendering the extremes of wet weather and drought of less frequent occurrence.

It is asserted by the inhabitants of the eastern parts of Kansas and Nebraska, that the rain-fall is more equally distributed through the seasons, and has increased in quantity since the settlement of the country. A similar change is noticed in the neighborhood of Denver, where the flow of small streams is more permanent. The waters of the Great Salt Lake, which twenty years ago appeared to be retroceding, have, it is said, risen seven feet since the Mormons established themselves in the valley. The exclusion of fires favors an increased growth of wood; orchards and shade trees are planted, and it seems probable that the substitution of the compact turf of cultivated grasses for the scattered bunch grass of the plains, is not without influence upon the atmosphere.

CHAPTER V.

CHANGE OF CLIMATE IN THE PRAIRIE REGIONS.

Since the advent of civilized man, and the general cultivation of the soil, considerable climatic changes have taken place in those parts of the Prairie countries which have been long settled. The most apparent of these changes are: First, greater aridity of the atmosphere. Second, more rapid evaporation. Third, greater irregularity of rain-fall. Fourth, diminished force of the prevailing winds. This statement is based on the observation and experience of a residence of forty years in Central and Northern Illinois. Although these changes are, with the exception of the last-mentioned, analogous to the effects produced in wooded countries by the removal of the forests, they cannot, in this instance, be ascribed to the same cause. As has before been said, the amount of timber was greater twenty years ago than at the first settlement of the country; and though the destruction has lately been rapid, the entire amount of woodland was originally so much less than that of prairie, that the diminution can as yet have had but little influence upon the climate.

The early settlers on the Illinois prairies found the dry uplands covered with a thick growth of native grass, of no great height except when seed stalks were thrown up, an occurrence which took place only once in two or three years. The scattered woodlands in Illinois, called *barrens*, produced a tall, thin growth of grass. On the low, flat prairie lands, the grass, mingled with sunflowers and other tall plants, mostly with composite flowers, was often from six to ten feet high, while the marshes and inundated bottom lands produced a coarse, reedy grass of great height. I remember riding near the Illinois river where, sitting on a horse sixteen hands high, I took the grass from each side and tied it together over the top of my hat.

In a great degree this rank vegetation, covering the whole country, compensated in its climatic influences for the paucity of forests. The rain falling on the surface of the earth, was retarded in passing off by the thick grass, and readily absorbed by the spongy soil. The rivulets with few exceptions spread out in wide beds called sloughs, having no well-defined channel, and, clothed with tall grass, slowly delivered their waters to the larger streams. The porous earth, unshorn of its vegetable growth throughout the growing season, yielded its moisture more gradually by evaporation than cultivated or pastured lands. In dry seasons, the deficiency of rain was in some measure supplied by copious dews. Rain almost uniformly fell in considerable quantity in the months of May and June, insuring a crop of grass and grain, even if the remainder of the season was dry.

Since the general appropriation of the soil to the use of civilized man, ponds and marshes, where the early settlers were wont to shoot waterfowl, have become dry land. The earth, rendered compact by cultivation and the tread of domestic animals, shorn of its vegetable covering, and nearly or quite bare for the whole or part of the Summer, absorbs less of the rain-fall, and parts with its moisture by evaporation more rapidly. Water from rain or melted snow is soon gathered into the channels washed out by the small streams, and speedily disappears from the face of the country. Extremes of wet and dry weather are more frequent, and the dews, condensed in dry seasons, are scanty. Instead of abundant rains in May and June, dry weather at that season is more common. A period of drought at the present day, commonly works far greater injury to crops than did a more protracted one in the early settlement of the country. These evils appear to be cumulative—to increase with the lapse of years. They may undoubtedly be mitigated, perhaps wholly removed, by planting a due proportion of the country with forest trees.

That the average force of the prevailing winds has diminished, or, as it is commonly expressed, the country is less windy than formerly, is a fact that must be recognized by all who have lived on the Illinois prairies thirty or forty years. The cause can only be found in the obstruction offered to the free passage of the wind by the orchards, shade trees, fences and buildings in the open country. If so few obstacles have a perceptible influence in this respect, there is good reason to suppose that a general planting of groves and belts of timber would essentially modify the climate.

CHAPTER VI.

PRACTICABILITY OF RAISING TIMBER.

The idea once common in the West, that as no trees were found upon the prairies, some natural incapacity for their production existed in the soil, has long since been exploded. Whatever may have been the origin of the prairies, experience has demonstrated that wherever the ravages of fire and pasturage by animals are prevented, young trees speedily spring up. Cornel and Sumach bushes, the Wild Crab and Wild Plum are usually the first to appear. These are followed by the Elm, Wild Cherry, and other trees with light seeds, which may be carried by the wind or transported by birds.

Mr. Marsh expresses the decided opinion that many parts even of the deserts of Asia and Africa would soon be covered with trees, if it were possible to prevent their destruction while small by the camels and goats of the wandering tribes. Where Nature, left undisturbed to her own operations, produces trees with facility, their cultivation by man cannot be difficult. Except in parts of the country which are still or have recently been covered with woods, the feeling once so common, that a forest tree was an object to be destroyed rather than cherished, has ceased to exist. The States of the Union most destitute of timber are taking the lead in forest culture, and it may well happen that fifty years hence these States will be better supplied with timber than those in which it originally most abounded.

Although the growth of forest trees has never been attempted by the great majority of the owners of the soil, it is neither difficult nor very expensive. Some kinds, the Black Walnut for example, may be planted and cultivated with as little trouble as the same number of acres of corn. Others must be sown in the seed-bed and transplanted. One objection made to planting trees for timber is the remoteness of the benefit to be derived from it—the long time it takes the trees to grow. It is true that he who plants forest trees can hardly expect to see them attain full maturity, yet he may in many ways derive from them great advantage, if not actual profit. Time plods on whether the trees grow or not. Groves and belts of woodland will in twenty years from planting—perhaps in less time—afford shade, protection, fencing, fuel and material for many other purposes. The man who cannot wait for the trees to grow, will perhaps see twenty years or more pass away, and at the last be destitute of the woods which might have been growing while he was sleeping.

There are in many parts of the country tracts of uneven land, generally near streams, which are partially or wholly covered with young trees. These tracts are usually among the least valuable for tillage, and should therefore be protected from devastation. Rivers, bluffs, ravines and steep slopes liable to wash under cultivation, are better suited to the growth of wood than to any other purpose.

Any farmer, although of small means, can plant at least an acre of trees in a year. When the ground for a grove or timber belt is selected, the outer rows may be first planted, and others added from year to year, as may be convenient. After the first three or four years, the trees will need little or no cultivation, and will require only pruning, thinning, and the exclusion of stock. Every farm of forty acres or more should have a proportion approximating to a fixed ratio of wood and tillage land. This ratio may be fixed at thirty acres of wood in a quarter section of one hundred and sixty acres, which is somewhat less than one-fifth. The proprietor whose farm consists wholly of arable land, may think this too much; yet a careful consideration of the subject must convince any intelligent person that the land cannot be put to a better use. If the plan were generally adopted of planting timber belts on the north and west sides of farms on open plains, protection would be afforded on the other two sides by neighboring plantations. A belt eight rods wide on two sides of a quarter section would give about the required proportion of thirty acres. In addition to other advantages, a farm, one-fifth of which was covered with thriving young trees, would always command a higher price and more ready sale than if it were destitute of wood.

A far greater variety of trees useful for timber is found in the United States than in Europe. In all parts of the Union, excepting the naked plains near the Rocky Mountains, are found valuable kinds suited to the soil and climate, seeds of which are easily procured.

CHAPTER VII.

PROPAGATION, PLANTING AND CULTURE.

It may be stated as a general rule, that the best and cheapest mode of growing forest trees for timber is by means of the seed. Most kinds of trees may be propagated by layers, many from cuttings; but the result is often the production of inferior trees. Exceptions may be found in the Willows, most if not all the Poplars, the Buttonwood, etc., which are most readily grown from cuttings. As no uniform mode of management can be practiced in gathering, preserving and planting the different kinds of tree seeds, their treatment will be best given in connection with the descriptions of the classes or species to which they belong.

To prepare the soil for the reception of seeds to be planted where the trees are to remain, or for young trees from the seed bed, the ground should be deeply ploughed and rendered mellow. It may then be marked out in rows four feet apart. If tall, straight timber is desired, the young trees must be planted thickly in the rows, and thinned as their growth requires. Acorns and nuts may be planted one foot apart; trees from the seed-bed two feet. When grown only for other purposes—for fuel, fruit, protection, etc., the distance may be varied to suit the object.

Where hillsides and slopes, not too steep to plough but likely to wash, are to be planted, it will be best to adopt the practice of cotton growers on uneven lands in the Southern States, there called *circling.* The ground is ploughed horizontally and the rows marked in the same direction, making curves where necessary, to correspond with the surface of the slope, and keeping all parts of each row as nearly as possible on the same level. By this management the danger of injury from washing by heavy rains is greatly lessened.

The sides of ravines and river bluffs, too steep for the use of the plough, may be planted with acorns, nuts or young trees, with the spade or garden-trowel. The European Larch is well suited to such localities. The vegetation in such situations is usually thin, and the turf not compact, and young trees will thrive there without cultivation better than on level lands.

Land for seed-beds should be deeply ploughed, and the soil well pulverized. If poor, it should be enriched with well-rotted manure. The seeds may be sown in narrow drills, twelve or fifteen inches apart, and covered from half an inch to one inch deep, according to size. If the ground be somewhat dry, a hand roller should be passed over it after sowing. It is best to sow as early in the spring as the ground can be got in good condition. Some seeds vegetate at a low temperature, and it is desirable that the plants should be growing well before hot dry weather occurs. The ground should be kept free from weeds, and frequently stirred between the drills during the summer. Such kinds of trees as make a growth of nine inches or more the first season, should be carefully taken up in the fall, their long roots shortened for convenience in replanting, and heeled in or buried, to be planted in spring where they are to remain. The labor of replanting is much less than when they are larger, and they are likely to make finer trees. Those which make but little growth the first year, may be left two or three years in the seed-bed. When this is done, they should be covered during the winter to prevent their being drawn out by the frost. A light covering of straw or coarse manure will answer the purpose.

After the young trees are planted where they are finally to remain, they should receive such cultivation as is bestowed upon a crop of corn. In ploughing among them, a short whiffletree, eighteen or twenty inches long, should be used to avoid injuring the trees. Weeds should be kept down in the autumn, as they afford shelter to mice. In November the rows should be ridged, which is done by turning a furrow against the trees on each side with a light plough. If one-half of the stems of the trees is covered, so much the better. Especially is this necessary the first season and upon level land. There is less danger that the plants will be drawn out by frost; water cannot collect around them in winter, and the ravages of mice are prevented. The ridges may easilv be leveled in spring with an iron rake, or with the cultivator. After three or four years, ploughing may be discontinued; and the plantation will, thenceforth, require little other care than pruning and thinning from time to time as may be needed.

As forest trees differ greatly in the rapidity of their growth, and the size to which they ultimately attain, it is best, as far as possible, to plant the different kinds separately. In a timber belt they may be disposed in squares or blocks. When planted promiscuously, the more rapid growers overpower the weaker. Evergreens and deciduous trees designed for timber, should not be mingled together in plantations.

The seeds of the Oaks, the Black Walnut, Butternut and the Hickories, most of which do not transplant well, should be planted where the trees are to remain. Trees, the seeds of which are small, or which make but little growth the first year, are best grown in seed-beds, until they are of proper size for transplanting.

For raising Willows or Poplars from cuttings, the slips should be not less than eight inches long, rejecting such as are less than one-third of an inch in diameter. They are best cut in autumn, and tied in small bundles with osier-withes or tarred twine. They may then be buried in the ground, selecting a spot not likely to become wet, or packed in damp earth and put in a cool place in the cellar. As early in the spring as practicable, they should be planted in a trench made with the plough or spade, placing them in an upright position, pressing the earth compactly around the lower part and leaving only an inch or two above ground. They are then to be cared for like seedlings.

Other modes of propagating forest trees—by layers, grafting, budding, etc., are employed by nurserymen and amateurs; but they would be of so little practical use to the great majority of those who may engage in forest culture, that their consideration here will be omitted.

CHAPTER VIII.

PRUNING AND THINNING.

Tree pruning is a subject that has been much discussed, and in regard to which there are various opinions; some even contending that trees should never be pruned at all. In the present case it will be considered only in relation to forest culture, without reference to amateur or ornamental cultivation. And here it may be premised, that in this as in other matters relating to tree growing, whatever rules may be given, the exercise of judgment and common sense is absolutely necessary, and must be employed in varying the practice to meet the circumstances of the case.

In pruning young trees, designed for timber, the symmetry of their form is the first consideration. When taken from the seed-bed all side branches should be cut off. Subsequently, an annual examination will be required to see that they grow in proper shape. Only one leading shoot should be allowed, which must not be permitted to fork. All side branches which approach in size and vigor to the leading shoot, should be shortened or cut out entirely. The Black Walnut, Butternut, Tulip tree and Chestnut are apt to throw out large side branches which take too much from the growth of the leading shoot. Suckers from the base of the tree should be cut away. Where suckers are thrown out in consequence of the stem of the tree being unthrifty or injured, the latter may be cut off, and one of the suckers allowed to take its place. In close plantations the trees may be trimmed up, two-thirds of their height, but too many branehes should not be taken off at once. Some kinds of trees require but little pruning. If properly treated while small, they will require less attention, in this respect, as they grow larger; and when their branches interlock, and their stems are thickly shaded, they will need little if any pruning. It should be always borne in mind that the main object in pruning forest trees is to give a proper direction to their growth. In an artificial plantation, properly managed, a great majority of the trees will be of value for timber; in a natural forest the reverse is usually the case; the greater part being fit only for firewood.

The best time to prune is, in my opinion, the autumn after the trees have ceased their growth. Where branches are taken off at this season, the wood hardens, and the wounds heal without decay. They may not heal as speedily as when the pruning is done in the growing season, but they heal better, which is, perhaps, more important. Side branches making a too rampant growth should be checked by clipping their ends during the summer; but any considerable amount of pruning at that season retards the growth of the trees. The worst time to prune is the latter part of winter, and in spring just before or during the first flow of sap. Trees pruned at this time bleed more or less; the wounds do not heal readily, and the wood, saturated with sap, is apt to decay. Nevertheless, when trees are transplanted in spring they may be pruned, as they do not bleed when recently taken up.

When the young trees become large enough to crowd, or materially check each other in growth, they must be thinned at one foot apart in the rows. Oaks and Hickories will grow to a proper size for hoop-poles before they will need thinning. When of this size they may be thinned so as to leave the remaining ones two feet apart. Care should be taken to leave the straightest and most vigorous trees. The thinning may be continued gradually as the trees grow larger, and those cut out, used for purposes to which their size and quality are adapted. The number of trees which will grow to maturity upon an acre, is from three hundred to four hundred. Larches, Pines and Spruces can be more thickly grown than most deciduous trees.

CHAPTER IX.

EXCLUSION OF ANIMALS FROM WOODLANDS.

Farm stock should not be permitted to range in woodlands at any season of the year, even after the trees have attained a considerable size. Not only is this important in respect to artificial plantations, but forests of natural growth, which are to be permanently devoted to the production of timber, should be kept closed against them. Any forest will in time be destroyed by a system of persistent pasturage. The undergrowth is entirely extirpated in a few years, and the young trees, upon which the continuation of the forest depends, are destroyed. Cattle soon learn to bend or break down slender trees even twenty feet high, and browse the leaves from their tops. The lower branches of the larger trees are stripped of their leaves and die. The growth of the wood is injuriously affected by the admission of cold and parching winds; by the trampling of cattle, which hardens the soil, and injures the roots of the trees, and by the close-fed turf, which forms wherever the shade is not too dense. From this combination of causes, some of the trees die, others are destroyed by the axe; and the thinning once commenced, goes on in an increasing ratio, as they are deprived of the accustomed protection afforded by close companionship. A case may be cited in point.

At the time of its first settlement, no part of the United States possessed more magnificent forests of the most valuable kinds of timber than Kentucky. After the country became thickly settled, the owners of valuable woodlands adopted the practice of cutting out the undergrowth and least valuable trees, and sowing the soil with blue grass. Beautiful indeed were these noble parks, shaded by lofty trees. Black Walnut, Oak, Ash, Tulip tree, Elm and Hackberry —carpeted with the soft turf of the blue grass, and pastured by herds of cattle. But the result was unfortunate. For more than twenty years past these noble trees have been rapidly perishing; no young ones have been permitted to grow to supply their place, and their reproduction, if ever accomplished, must be effected by means of artificial plantations. I am informed by a gentleman, a native of Kentucky, that in some parts of that State coal for fuel is, at the present time, conveyed sixty miles in wagons.

With proper management and protection, a forest will continue to reproduce itself for an indefinite period of time. Nature, if left to herself, will carry on her operations successfully; if not assisted, they must at least be unchecked.

CHAPTER X.

SCREENS FOR SHELTER.

When timber belts are planted on the outskirts of the farm, it may often happen that they will be too remote from the farm buildings to afford the needed protection. In such cases, it will be desirable to plant screens consisting of one or more rows of trees. These should be evergreens, as deciduous trees in a belt so narrow would afford but little shelter at the season when it is most needed. A single row of evergreens, when well grown, is a very good protection against the winter wind. A double row is still better. Two rows of Norway Spruce, planted eight or ten feet apart, and ten feet distant in the rows, each tree being opposite the space in the other row, constitute as complete a shelter from the wind as a building of the same height. The evergreens most suitable for screens are, the Norway Spruce, the White Pine, the Red Pine, Scotch Pine and Austrian Pine. The American Arbor Vitæ, Hemlock, White and Black Spruce, are also well suited for this purpose, but do not grow so rapidly as those first mentioned. Orchards not otherwise protected, should have screens planted near them. Experience has shown that sheltered orchards, other things being equal, are the most productive; besides, their fruit is less likely to be shaken from the trees by violent winds.

Cattle should be carefully debarred all access to evergreens, as they are fond of amusing themselves by twisting and breaking the branches with their horns. In making forest plantations on the plains towards the Rocky Mountains, the propriety of previously planting screens of Cottonwood and White Willow for their protection has been suggested. It seems quite likely that this may be found expedient, if not necessary. These trees, particularly the Cottonwood, are more hardy when young than many of the more valuable kinds of timber, and may answer a good purpose in sheltering them from the scorching winds which, in Summer, sweep over those regions. Both are easily grown from cuttings, which should be set as early in the Spring as practicable. The Cottonwood is found on the banks of streams everywhere throughout the West, and is therefore easily obtained.

The best method of managing tree plantations on the Western plains is, however, yet to be learned by experience. The practicability of raising timber in that region can scarcely be doubted, since it seems certain that where grass will grow trees may be made to grow also.

CHAPTER XI.

PROFIT OF TIMBER CULTURE.

In estimating the profits of timber culture in the United States, all calculations must of necessity be prospective, and without the pretence of exactness, since no one can foresee what may be the value of timber when the increasing demand, and the consequent rapid destruction of the forests, shall have produced the scarcity which is inevitable. It is the general opinion of those who have considered the subject, that lands in the rural districts planted with valuable timber will, in twenty-five years from the present time, be of greater value than any other. Some of the best kinds of timber thrive upon very poor soils, or on rocky and broken lands, so that tracts almost worthless for any other purpose may, by covering them with trees, be rendered the most valuable part of an estate. The Larch plantations of the Duke of Athol, in Scotland, were made upon land worth from ninepence to one shilling per acre. At thirty years from planting, the trees were thinned to four hundred per acre, which was considered the proper number to grow to a large size. The value at different ages was estimated as follows:

400 trees per acre, at	30	years old	-	$375
400 " "	43	"	-	2,250
400 " "	59	"	-	10,000
400 " "	72	"	-	15,000

It is not, however, necessary to wait thirty years for profit from a forest plantation. Many kinds of timber yield a return long before the expiration of that time. The early thinnings of Oak, Hickory, Ash, Chesnut and Birch plantations may be employed for hoop-poles, and when too large for that purpose are of value for many other uses.

The European Larch, grown thickly, affords long, slender poles, which are useful for fencing and very durable; it is also used for hop-poles and grape-stakes. Grown four feet apart—about two thousand seven hundred trees on an acre—the Larch will in a few years become large enough for fence posts. Round Cedar posts (Arbor Vitæ) sell in Chicago for from twenty-two to fifty cents each. The Larch is, if the testimony of European writers may be believed, even more durable than the Arbor Vitæ. The following table, drawn up by D. C. Scofield, of Elgin, Illinois, shows the size attained in twelve years by forest trees planted by himself. The land where the trees grow is dry prairie; the soil loamy, the subsoil clayey loam, underlaid with gravel at a depth of from six to ten feet. The plants when set were from six to twelve inches high, and their size, after twelve years' growth, was ascertained by actual measurement.

	Diameter.	Height.
European Larch -	8 to 12 inches.	30 feet.
Black or Am. Larch	4 " 6 "	25 "
White Ash - -	3 " 5 "	16 "
Silver Maple - -	4 " 6 "	25 "
Sugar Maple - -	2 " 4 "	12 "
Black Walnut -	2 " 4 "	14 "
Chestnut - - -	3 " 4 "	16 "
White Elm - -	3 " 4 "	16 "
Scotch Elm - -	3 " 4 "	16 "
European Birch -	4 " 6 "	14 "
European Beech -	2 " 4 "	10 "
White Pine - -	6 " 10 "	35 "
Norway Spruce - -	5 " 8 "	20 "
Scotch Pine - -	4 " 8 "	20 "
Austrian Pine - -	5 " 7 "	16 "
Balsam Fir - -	4 " 6 "	16 "

The above is not a solitary instance of the rapid growth of the Larch in the West. We may therefore assume that it can be grown in twelve years to such size that each tree will furnish two fence posts. Allowing four hundred trees to remain to become of larger size, and deducting three hundred for those worthless or indifferent, two thousand trees might be cut from an acre, affording 4,000 posts, which, valued at only twenty cents each, would be worth eight hundred dollars. The upper part of the trees might be used for rails to nail on the fence posts, or for other purposes. The estimate of twenty cents each for the posts is much below what they would be worth in many parts of the country at the present time. The railroads annually require an immense number of ties, and no kind of timber is better fitted for that use than the Larch.

Those who regard only immediate profit, and look solely to the most expeditious way of realizing money, from an undertaking, will not be likely to plant timber. But those who are willing to wait, or who desire to make a profitable investment for their children, cannot engage in any enterprise with greater certainty of ultimate advantage than forest planting. The immense consumption of timber, annually increasing with our increasing population — the multiplied uses for which the more valuable kinds are indispensable—the wide plains towards the Rocky Mountains rapidly filling with emigrants, who must long be wholly or in part dependent on remote districts for their supplies, render it absolutely certain that the price of timber must in a few years be greatly enhanced.

CHAPTER XII.

DESCRIPTION OF INDIVIDUAL DECIDUOUS TREES.

Acer—Maple. Natural Order, Aceraceæ.

Flowers, polygamous; calyx, five-lobed, colored; petals, five or none; stamens, four to twelve; ovary, two-celled, with a pair of ovules in each; styles, two. Leaves pulmately lobed and toothed. Seeds in pairs, each furnished with a wing.

The Maples generally belong to northern latitudes, and are capable of enduring an intense degree of cold. Some of the species are lofty trees and all are beautiful. The wood is useful in the arts and in domestic economy. Its quality, however, differs so widely in the different species, that it cannot be characterized by general remarks.

1. *Acer dasycarpum—Silver Maple, White Maple, Soft Maple.*

Leaves deeply five-lobed, the sinuses rather acute; silvery-white underneath; lobes unequally and deeply toothed. Flowers, greenish or reddish-yellow, without petals, appearing before the leaves. Seeds downy while young, with large divergent wings.

The Silver Maple is found on the banks of rivers from Maine to Georgia, though it is less common near either extreme than in intermediate latitudes. It is abundant along the Western rivers. According to Michaux, trees twelve or fifteen feet in circumference were common in his time along the banks of the Ohio. Its ordinary height may be stated at fifty or sixty feet, with a diameter of two feet.

The rapid growth, graceful branches and fine silvery foliage of this tree have induced its extensive planting for ornament and shade. It is, however, liable to be broken by high winds, and by ice or snow accumulating on the branches. When closely planted in groves or belts, this is less likely to occur. I know no forest tree, except, perhaps, the Box Elder, that will make so speedy a return of equally valuable wood for fuel as the Silver Maple. It is preferred to Oak for kitchen fuel, particularly for summer use. It is used in the manufacture of Windsor chairs, and for some other purposes. I have seen floors made of it which were esteemed for their smoothness and ease of cleaning. The wood is fine grained, but light and of little strength or durability.

The seeds ripen in two or three weeks after the leaves are fully developed, and must be gathered and sown soon after. They are usually planted in drills about one inch deep. If the ground is dry it should be rolled after sowing. The plants will appear in from six to ten days. If very hot, dry weather occurs soon after sowing, the young plants are apt to be scorched by the sun as they emerge from the soil.

The whole sowing is sometimes lost from this cause. This may be prevented by shading the rows with branches of trees, or by lightly covering them with straw or hay, to be removed when the danger is past.

The trees will grow from one to two feet the first season. Under very favorable circumstances they sometimes double this. If designed for plantations they are best removed when one year old; or, if sown where they are to remain, they should be thinned at that age. With ordinary care the Silver Maple transplants as successfully as any other tree.

2. *Acer rubrum—Red Maple, Soft Maple.*

Leaves, three to five-lobed, unequally notched, whitish beneath; flowers red; petals, five, linear oblong; capsules, smooth; seeds, red.

The Red Maple is found mostly in swamps or moist lands from Canada to the Gulf of Mexico. When full grown it is a large tree, sixty or seventy feet high, and two or three feet in diameter. It is often confounded with the Silver Maple, which it somewhat resembles. The flowers, which appear two or three weeks before the leaves, are of a beautiful purple or deep red. The leaves change to different shades of red in the fall, even before frost. The wood is harder and finer grained than that of the Silver Maple. It is suitable for turning, and is applied to a variety of uses in the manufacture of furniture. The variety called Curled Maple, which is frequently in this species, is much used for the stocks of fowling pieces and rifles.

East of the Alleghanies, the Red Maple appears to be much more common than the Silver Maple. I have never found it in Central or Northern Illinois, although it is said to grow in some localities. Further south it is common. It is scarcely probable that it will ever be much cultivated for any other purpose than as a beautiful ornamental tree.

The seeds, which are red, and only about half as large as those of the Silver Maple, are ripe about the same time. They are sown and treated in the same manner.

3. *Acer saccharinum—Sugar Maple, Rock Maple.*

Leaves, three to five-lobed, paler beneath; flowers, greenish-yellow, in clusters, pendulous; petals, none; wings of the fruit broad, slightly diverging.

The Sugar Maple is by far the most valuable species of its genus, and it is, also, the most abundant in that part of the United States which lies north of latitude 40,° and east of the Mississippi river. Southward it is found chiefly on the mountains, and it becomes rare in going westward from the Mississippi. This species is often found of the height of seventy or eighty feet, with a diameter of three feet; but is commonly of less size. The wood is hard, heavy and strong, but not durable when exposed to the weather. As fuel, it ranks next to the Hickory. It is fine grained and has a silky lustre when polished. It is employed in cabinet work, the gearing of mills, and in naval architecture. The undulations and inflections of fibre called Curled Maple and Bird's-eye

Maple, are used in veneering articles of furniture, and are highly esteemed.

The use of the sap of the Sugar Maple in the production of sugar is well known. In Vermont, New Hampshire, and other parts of the country, considerable quantities are annually manufactured, some individuals making, in a favorable season, three thousand or four thousand pounds. It is sold at a higher price than sugar made from the cane. Syrup made from the sap of the Maple is esteemed superior to any other.

The seeds of the Sugar Maple ripen about the first of October. Like those of other Maples, they are in pairs, united at the base, and furnished with a wing. Their external appearance is precisely similar; but, upon examination, I have uniformly found one of each pair abortive and worthless. The trees rarely, if ever, produce seed two years in succession. The seed may be sown in autumn, or mixed with sand and kept damp—never wet—through the winter in a place cool enough to prevent vegetation. It should be sown early in spring, in drills as directed for the Silver Maple. The young plants grow slowly for the first two or three years, and may remain two years in the seed-bed.

The Sugar Maple should never be planted on low flat lands, with a retentive subsoil, unless it is underdrained. It will not live where the soil is saturated with water during the growing season. In such situations a single wet summer is sufficient to destroy it. In the very wet summer of 1844, I lost a number of

Acer Platanoides—Norway Maple.

Sugar Maples which had been growing several years upon land which, in an ordinary season, was dry enough for cultivation. Poor sandy soils are not suited to the growth of the Sugar Maple. It will thrive on almost any good tillage land, and flourishes on the banks of ravines and the sides of bluffs and hills.

The Sugar Maple was strongly recommended by Michaux, for propagation in the North of Europe, as superior to any other species. It certainly merits cultivation in its native country, both for its utility and beauty. Its slow growth in its early stages should not discourage its propagation, since it continues to increase in size at an age when the Silver Maple is nearly stationary.

4. *Acer nigrum—Black Sugar Maple.*

Leaves, three to five-lobed, larger and less bayed and cut than the preceding species; slightly downy beneath; leaf stalks shorter and stouter.

This tree, formerly described as a distinct species, is now generally considered a variety of A. saccharinum. Its growth and general appearance are similar, but its leaves are larger, less scolloped and darker colored. The whole tree is darker in appearance, whence it derives its name. The essential characteristics of its wood and sap are so nearly like those of the Common Sugar Maple as not to require a separate description. It is propagated in the same manner. Some assert that it is to be preferred for the production of sugar. My own experience does not enable

5

me to decide this point. It is considered by many a more ornamental tree than the Common Sugar Maple.

5. *Acer negundo (Negundo aceroides.)—Box Elder, Ash-leaved Maple.*

Leaves, pinnate and ternate, unequally serrate; flowers, diœcious; calyx, four to five-cleft; petals, none; stamens, four to five.

This species, in favorable situations, becomes a stately tree, reaching the height of fifty or sixty feet. It is most common along the banks of streams. It is very hardy, being abundant about the Red River of the North as far as latitude 54.° In rich soil its prowth when young is astonishingly rapid, even surgassing that of the Silver Maple. In very dry soil it is short lived. Sugar may be made from its sap, which is abundant. This, and its very rapid growth, have induced some to recommend its culture for the production of sugar. The quality of its wood is similar to that of the Silver and Red Maples. It is a beautiful ornamental tree with dense foliage, and, when standing singly, a round symmetrical head. Its rapid growth renders it desirable for planting where it is an object to produce an effect in the shortest possible time. The seed, a large proportion of which is sometimes abortive, ripens in the fall, and is treated like that of the Sugar Maple.

6. *Acer Pennsylvanicum—Moose wood, Striped Maple.*

Leaves, three-lobed at the apex; double serrate; the short lobes taper-pointed and also serrate;

racemes drooping, loose; petals, obovate; fruit with diverging wings.

The Striped Maple is a small tree, seldom exceeding the height of thirty feet, and frequently not more than half that stature. It is found in northern woods from Maine to Wisconsin, and southward along the summits of the Alleghanies. It has heavy, dense foliage, and smooth light-green bark, striped longitudinally with dark lines. The wood is more durable than that of other species of Maple, but is too small for use. It is worthy of notice only as a highly ornamental tree. If grafted on larger species of Maple, it is said to reach three or four times its ordinary size. It is propagated from seed in the same manner as the Sugar Maple.

7. *Acer spicatum—the Mountain Maple,*

Is a still smaller tree, very ornamental; and may, also, be increased in size by grafting on larger species.

8. *Acer platanoides—Norway Maple.*

Leaves, milky, broadly cordate, five-lobed, coarsely toothed; fruit, diverging; flowers, pendulous.

This species is a native of the north of Europe, and grows to the height of sixty feet or more. It considerably resembles the Sugar Maple, and, like that, produces sap from which sugar is made. It is of slow growth for the first three or four years from the seed, but afterwards increases in size rapidly. As an ornamental tree it has some advantages over the Sugar Maple; its foliage is more dense, its leaves appear earlier in spring, and retain their verdure later in the fall; but in the production of sap, and the quality of its timber, it is inferior to the American tree. It is propagated from seed like the Sugar Maple.

9. *Acer pseudoplatanus—Sycamore Maple.*

Leaves, heart-shaped, smooth; five-lobed, unequally toothed; racemes, pendulous; fruit, smooth, with long, large wings.

The Sycamore Maple is a native of of the Eastern Continent, but has for many years been cultivated as an ornamental tree in the older States of the Union. It attains the height of sixty feet. It is a rather coarse growing tree, with stiff branches. The wood is esteemed in Europe for turning, and is applied to a variety of other uses. It is, however, inferior to that of the Sugar Maple, and the tree is not likely to be much noticed by any but amateurs. The young seedlings are sometimes injured by the winter in Northern Illinois, but after a few years become quite hardy. They do not transplant successfully when several years old. The seeds ripen in October, and are treated like those of other species.

AESCULUS—HORSE CHESTNUT, BUCKEYE.

Natural Order, Sapindaceæ.

Calyx tubular, five-lobed; petals, four or five, unequal; stamens, seven; filaments long and slender, often unequal; seed large, with a shining coat and a large, round, pale scar.

Aesculus hippocastanum—Horse Chestnut.

Corolla spreading, white, spotted with purple and yellow; petals, five; stamens declined; leaflets, seven.

This is a large tree, sometimes reaching the height of eighty feet. It is a native of Northern Asia, and is cultivated in this country only for ornament. In soils which suit it, it grows rapidly, but I have never known it to thrive on the Illinois prairies. The wood is soft and of little value, although applied to some uses in Europe. The nuts, ground and mixed with feed, are said to be a palliative, if not a cure, for broken-winded horses. The seeds must not be allowed to become dry previous to sowing. They may be planted in autumn, and covered with litter, to be taken off in spring, or buried through the winter where they will not become too wet.

Aesculus glabra—Ohio Buckeye.

Stamens curved, much longer than the pale yellow corolla; petals, four, upright; fruit, prickly; leaflets, five.

The Ohio Buckeye is commonly a small tree, but often attains the height of forty or fifty feet. It is one of the earliest trees to put forth its leaves, and flowers in spring, and is then very handsome; but it loses its foliage very early, sometimes in August. As a timber tree, it is one of the most worthless. Cattle are said to be sometimes killed by gorging themselves with the nuts.

Aesculus flava—Sweet Buckeye.

Stamens included in the yellow corolla; petals, four; calyx, oblong, campanulate; leaflets five, sometimes seven; smooth or minutely downy beneath; fruit, smooth.

The Sweet Buckeye is a stately tree, growing only in the richest soils, and reaching the height of sixty or seventy feet, with a diameter of three or four feet. It belongs to the subgenus Pavia, the husk of the fruit being smooth instead of prickly, like that of Horse Chestnut. Its bark and wood are nearly destitute of the disagreeable odor of the preceding species—hence the name of Sweet Buckeye. Its flowers and foliage are handsome, but it is usually bare of leaves by the first of September, which renders it unfit for ornamental purposes. The only use I have ever known to be made of its timber was for the construction of log cabins and the manufacture of wooden bowls. It is common from Northern Illinois southward. It may be propagated like the Horse Chestnut.

Aesculus Pavia—The Red Buckeye,

Common in rich bottom lands in the Southern States, is the handsomest species. It has large, showy spikes of bright red flowers, but is little more than a shrub. It is said to be hardy at the North.

AILANTUS.

Natural Order, Rutaceæ.

Calyx, five-cleft; petals, five; stamens, ten, unequal; styles, three to five, arising from the notches of the ovaries; carpels, three to five, membraneous; one-celled; one-seeded.

Ailantus glandulosa—Ailantus.

Leaves unequally pinnate, the leaflets coarsely toothed at the base, the teeth glandulous on the under side.

This tree is a native of the Northern Provinces of China, and was introduced into the United States many years since. It was at one time planted to some extent for ornament and shade, but its disposition to sucker, and the offensive odor of its flowers, rendered it unpopular. It becomes a large tree, reaching the height of sixty or seventy feet. For the first ten or twelve years it grows with great rapidity, but afterwards more slowly. The wood is hard and fine grained, and is well fitted for cabinet work. It is also good fuel. It has been largely planted of late on the steppes in the south of Russia, and is said to be well fitted to fasten loose, blowing sands. In France it grows to a large size on chalky soils, where few other trees will live. It has been recommended for planting on the arid plains of Western Kansas. In Northern Illinois it is sometimes killed by severe winters. It is easily propagated by seeds, suckers and cuttings of the roots.

AMELANCHIER—JUNEBERRY.

Natural Order, Rosaceæ.

Calyx, five-cleft; petals, oblong, elongated; stamens numerous, short; styles, five, united below; fruit, berry-like.

Amelanchier Canadensis—Shadbush, Service-berry.

Calyx-lobes triangular, lanceform; fruit, globular, purplish, edible; ripe in June.

The greatest height attained by this tree is thirty or forty feet, with a diameter of ten or twelve inches, but it is commonly of much smaller size. It grows in most parts of the United States, and is said to be most abundant on the Alleghany Mountains. It is a handsome tree, blooming profusely early in the season. Its flowers are white, and are produced in long panicles. The fruit is palatable, but is seldom abundant, and is greedily devoured by birds when scarcely ripe. It merits notice only as an ornamental tree. There are several varieties, some of them dwarfish. It is easily propagated from seed.

ASIMINA PAPAW.

Natural Order, Anonaceæ.

Petals, six, increasing after the bud opens, the outer set larger than the inner; stamens, numerous, in a globular mass; pistils, few, ripening one to three large and oblong, pulpy, several seeded fruits; seeds horizontal, flat.

Asimina triloba—Papaw.

Leaves thin, obovate, lanceolate, pointed; petals, dull purple, veiny, round-ovate, the outer ones three to four times as long as the calyx.

The Papaw is commonly only a large shrub, but often reaches the height of twenty or thirty feet, with a diameter of six or eight inches. It is found from

Western New York to Northern Illinois and southward, growing mostly on rich bottom lands. Its presence is a certain indication of a soil of great fertility. The leaves are large, the flowers dark purple. The fruit is oblong, with a pulp somewhat resembling egg custard in consistence and taste. Some people are fond of it, but it is too luscious for the taste of many. The trees seldom produce fruit near the northern limit of their growth.

The wood is soft, spongy, and of no value. As an ornamental tree, the beauty of its flowers and foliage recommend it to the notice of cultivators.

BETULA—BIRCH.

Natural Order, Betulaceæ.

Sterile catkins long and drooping, terminal and lateral, formed in summer, and expanding their golden flowers in early spring, preceding the leaves; fertile catkins, oblong or cylindrical, lateral, protected by scales through the winter, and developed with the leaves; seeds with a membranous edge; foliage mostly thin and light.

The Birches described in this work are, with one or two exceptions, found mostly in northern latitudes, and are best suited to cold climates, or elevated situations. Excepting the Red, and, perhaps, the Black Birch, they are not likely to be ever much cultivated south of latitude 40°.

Small plants of the Yellow Birch and Canoe Birch can be cheaply obtained from the forests of Northern Wisconsin and Michigan. When this can be done, it will be better than to attempt raising them from seed. With ordinary care, they transplant, when small, with ease and certainty of success. If seeds are bought, care should be taken to get only those which have been freshly gathered.

The Birches are all fine trees, and in all parts of the country are desirable to those who wish for variety in their plantations.

1. *Betula lenta—Black Birch, Cherry Birch.*

Leaves heart-ovate, sharply and finely double serrate, hairy on the veins beneath; fruiting catkins elliptical, thick, somewhat hairy; lobes of the veiny scales nearly equal, obtuse, diverging.

When full grown, the Black Birch is sixty or seventy feet high, and two or three feet in diameter. It is one of the handsomest of the Birches, and the most valuable for timber. It is found from New England to Ohio; northward to Canada, and southward along the mountains. The bark and twigs are highly aromatic. The wood is of a rosy hue; it is fine grained, and is esteemed next to the Wild Cherry for cabinet work. It is also excellent fuel. It will thrive in soils and situations that suit the Sugar Maple, and is well worthy cultivation. The seeds are ripe about the first of November, and should be mixed with sand and kept till spring. They should be sown in beds of light, sandy loam, and very thinly covered. They will germinate better if slightly covered with moss or leaves to keep the surface moist.

2. *Betula excelsa—Yellow Birch.*

Leaves ovate or elliptical, pointed, smoothish, unequally serrate; fertile catkins, ovoid, oblong, slightly hairy; lobes of the scales nearly equal, acute, diverging slightly.

Notwithstanding its specific name of *excelsa*, this tree does not exceed some other species of Birch in stature. It is a beautiful tree, sometimes sixty or seventy feet high, with a straight trunk of nearly uniform diameter for thirty or forty feet. In open ground its branches are numerous, forming a conical head. Its twigs are aromatic, but less so than those of the Black Birch. It is a northern tree, growing in cool, moist, and sometimes in wet lands. It thrives well on the Illinois prairies, but is not adapted to dry, sandy, or gravelly soils. Fuller says the wood is of little value. It is nevertheless considered excellent fuel where it grows; it is strong, fine grained, proper for turning, and makes handsome furniture, though inferior for that purpose to the Black Birch. The seeds ripen in October, and are treated like those of the preceding species.

3. *Betula nigra—Red Birch, River Birch.*

Leaves rhombic-obovate, acutish at both ends, whitish and downy underneath; fertile catkins, oblong, woolly.

When full grown, this is a lofty tree, seventy feet high, and two feet in diameter. The specific name *nigra* is of unfortunate application to this species, since the B. lenta is every way darker in appearance, and is known as Black Birch wherever it grows. The epithet *rubra*, applied to it by Michaux, best designates the appearance of the Red Birch, but is discarded by most botanists.

The Red Birch is found only on the banks of rivers, but will thrive in other localities. Of all the Birches, this is found in the warmest latitudes, and it is doubtless best adapted to cultivation south of latitude 40°. Its wood is similar in quality to that of the Yellow Birch. The seeds ripen in the beginning of June, and must be sown immediately, and the young plants shaded from the sun as they come up.

4. *Betula papyracea—Canoe Birch.*

Leaves, ovate, taper-pointed, heart-shaped or abrupt at the base; smooth above, dull underneath.

The Canoe Birch is a northern tree, found from New England to Wisconsin, and northward. It is rarely, if ever, met with south of latitude 42°. It grows to the height of seventy feet, with a diameter of three feet. It is said to be found eighteen or twenty feet in circumference in the British possessions near the Red and Saskatchewan rivers. The bark is of a brilliant white, and is used by the Indians and fur traders of the north in the construction of canoes. It is easily divided into thin sheets, and constitutes a principal material in the "Indian fancy work" sold at Niagara, and other places of fashionable resort.

The Canoe Birch is a beautiful ornamental tree, and will thrive in soils that are too wet for the Black Birch and Sugar Maple. It affords excellent firewood,

Betula Papyracea—Papery-barked Birch.

and is worth cultivating where that is an object. It grows rapidly on rich prairie soil. The seed ripens about the middle of July, and may be treated like that of the Black Birch.

5. *Betula alba—European White Birch.*

Leaves, ovate, acute, somewhat triangular, unequally serrate, nearly smooth.

This species, which is cultivated for ornament in this country, is, in the north of Europe, a lofty tree, reaching, according to Michaux, the height of seventy or eighty feet. In the south of Europe it is smaller, and the timber inferior; while in the extreme north it becomes a shrub. In the spring it yields abundance of sap, from which a rich syrup may be made; but it will not crystallize. In the countries where it is native, it is applied to a great variety of uses. Its only advantage over the Canoe Birch is its capability of thriving in the most barren soils, where scarcely anything else will grow. It is propagated like the preceding species. There are some varieties, of which the cut-leaved is the most beautiful. This is propagated by layers or cuttings.

6. *Betula populifolia—American White Birch.*

Leaves, triangular, very taper-pointed, truncate, or nearly so, at the broad base; smooth and shining both sides.

This is a small tree, common near the coast from Maine to Pennsylvania. It springs up in waste, barren lands, old worn-out pastures, and along fences. Its wood is soft and speedily decays. It is a graceful ornamental tree, which is its only claim to notice, its wood being of the poorest quality even for fuel. It is now considered by botanists a variety of the preceding species.

CARYA—HICKORY.

Natural Order, Juglandaceæ.

Sterile flowers, in lateral catkins, which are mostly in threes, on a common peduncle; stamens, three to eight; fertile flowers, two or three together at the end of the branches; calyx, four-toothed; petals, none; fruit, globular, with a fleshy and, at length, leathery bark, which splits into four valves, and falls away from the nut; leaves, odd pinnate, five to fifteen leaflets, the two sorts of flowers from the same scaly buds with these; the sterile catkins borne below the leaves.

The Hickory, common in most parts of the United States, is exclusively an American tree. The different species grow in a variety of soils, but resemble each other in the qualities of their timber. So close is the resemblance, that no difference can be detected in the grain or color of the wood. They are all heavy, and combine, though in different degrees, the qualities of hardness, strength, and elasticity. They have also in common the disadvantages of speedy decay when exposed to heat and moisture, and peculiar liability to injury from worms. So important are the uses of the Hickory, that it would be difficult, if not impossible, to find another tree that would supply its place.

As fuel, Hickory wood is more esteemed than any other in the market, either in America or Europe; and is made the standard of value with which other wood is compared. It produces a strong heat, and leaves a heavy, compact, and lasting coal. The difference of the species in value for fuel is not great, though the Shellbark and Mockernut are considered the best, and Bitternut the poorest. For making hoops, the Hickory is better adapted than any other tree.

The Hickories all ripen their nuts at the same time, and they receive the same treatment in propagation. When the nuts are gathered, they may be laid in heaps on a spot of dry ground, remote from the haunts of rats or mice, and covered with turf peeled from the soil around, adding three or four inches of earth above it. If the turf be wanting, a covering of straw may supply its place. The turf or straw will prevent the inconvenience caused by mixing earth with the nuts. In spring they may be planted as directed in the chapter on Propagation. As the Hickory does not transplant well, it is best, if possible, to plant where the trees are to remain, and in this case it is proper to plant two nuts where one is expected to grow. It is cheaper to destroy those that are superfluous, than to fill vacancies by transplanting. If, however, they are to be removed, it should be done when one year old, since the earlier they are established in their final locality the better trees they will become. Michaux recommends causing them to germinate in boxes filled with earth, and kept moist in the cellar, the success of which, he says, is certain. If this plan be adopted, care must be taken that they are kept so cool as not to sprout too early for planting. Some advise planting in the fall, but I have never succeeded, even tolerably well, in this way. The nuts are likely to be discovered and taken out by mice and squirrels, which, if they once find them, show great pertinacity and some cunning in hunting them up. The young trees should receive clean culture until they are no longer in danger of being smothered by weeds.

The Hickories are all of rather slow growth, which renders it more important that the young trees, of which there are many in some parts of the country, should be spared by the axe, and protected from cattle.

1. *Carya alba—Shellbark Hickory.*

Leaflets, five; minutely downy underneath; finely serrate; the three upper obovate lanceolate; the lower pair much smaller, and oblong lanceolate; all taper-pointed; fruit, depressed; globular; nut, somewhat flattened, nearly pointless, with a rather thin whitish shell, and a large kernel.

This species when full grown is a lofty tree, but is, proportionally, less in diameter than most other trees. It is often eighty feet high with a diameter of two feet or less. The trunk is of uniform diameter and destitute of branches for the greater part of its height. It is one of the most valuable of the Hickories for timber, and is not surpassed by any other tree for fuel.

Most of the Hickory nuts of commerce are the fruit of this species. The large trees are remarkable for the exfoliation of the outer bark, which is divided into long narrow plates, adhering by the middle or one end. No species of Hickory better merits cultivation than this. When young, it is a graceful ornamental tree, and were it of foreign origin it would be cultivated for its beauty. The fruit varies considerably in quantity and size, and may, undoubtedly, be improved by cultivation. If planted with a view to the production of fruit, only the best varieties should be selected. It was long ago asserted as a fact, that Hickory trees which had been transplanted were best for the production of fruit, although inferior for timber. I have never seen this statement verified by trial, but it appears quite probable. Michaux, in the *North American Sylva,* mentions a variety of the Shellbark Hickory, produced on a farm at Seacocus near Snake Hill, in New Jersey, with nuts nearly twice as large as any that he had seen elsewhere; and remarked that, perhaps, a century of cultivation would not advance the species generally to an equal degree of perfection. It is said that the fruit of the European Walnut (Juglans regia), in its uncultivated state, is inferior, both in size and quality, to that of the Shellbark Hickory.

2. *Carya sulcata—Thick Shellbark Hickory.*

Leaflets, seven or nine; obovate lanceolate; sharply serrate; downy underneath; fruit, oval; four-ribbed above the middle, with intervening furrows; nut, strongly pointed, slightly flattened, with a thick yellowish shell.

The Thick Shellbark Hickory is said to be much less common east of the Alleghanies than in the Western States. It is a lofty tree, and is sometimes confounded with the preceding species, which it resembles in the quality of its timber and the exfoliation of its bark. The leaves are, also, similar, but differ in being composed of seven or nine leaflets instead of five, which is always the number of the Shellbark Hickory. The nut of this species is very different from that of the other; it is nearly twice as large, is longer than it is broad, and has a firm point at each end. The shell is of a yellowish color, thick and hard, and the kernel of inferior flavor.

3. *Carya tomentosa—Mockernut.*

Leaflets, seven or nine; oblong, or obovate lanceolate; slightly serrate; roughish downy underneath, as well as the petiole; catkins, hairy; fruit, globular, or ovoid, with a thick, hard husk which splits almost to the base; nut, somewhat six-angled; the shell very thick and hard; light-brown color.

The Mockernut Hickory grows to the height of fifty or sixty feet, with a diameter of eighteen or twenty inches. It is not rare, though not abundant in Northern Illinois; and appears to be more multiplied east of the Alleghanies than in the western country. The bark on old trees is thick, hard and rugged. The wood is considered among the best for strength and toughness, as well as for fuel. The shell of the nut is very thick, and extremely hard; the kernel is sweet but small, and difficult to extract; hence, probably, the name of Mockernut.

According to Michaux, who proved the fact by actual experiment, this species is of the slowest growth of all the Hickories. This consideration will, probably, induce cultivators to prefer some other species for propagation.

4. *Carya glabra—Pignut Hickory.*

Leaflets, five or seven; ovate lanceolate; serrate, smooth; fruit, pear-shaped, or roundish obovate; husk, thin, splitting about half way down, and generally adhering when the nut falls; nut, hard and tough; kernel, small, sweet or bitterish.

In the southern parts of New England, and in the Middle States towards the Atlantic coast, the Pignut is one of the most multiplied of the Hickories. It appears to be less common in the Western States. It is a large tree, growing to the height of seventy or eighty feet, with a diameter of three or four feet. The wood is considered by many the strongest and toughest of the Hickories, and is preferred where it grows, for axletrees and axe handles. The nuts serve only as food for animals and are never taken to market.

5. *Carya olivæformis—Pecan-nut.*

Nearly smooth; leaflets, thirteen or fifteen; oblong lanceolate; serrate; somewhat falcate; nut, olive-shaped with a thin shell.

The Pecan tree is found principally, if not exclusively, upon river bottoms, from Northern Illinois to Texas. It is a stranger to the Atlantic States. It most resembles the Bitternut Hickory and will thrive in the same soils. On the Illinois river it is found as far north as Lacon, and on the Mississippi as high as latitude 42.°

The Pecan grows in the forest to the height of sixty or seventy feet. It is a beautiful tree, with a straight and well-shaped trunk. Its timber is inferior to that of some of the species already described, but it merits the attention of the cultivator on account of the excellence of its fruit. No other nut, native or imported, can be compared with it in flavor. The shell is thin, the kernel destitute of woody partitions, and easily extracted, By cultivation and the selection of superior varieties for propagation, the fruit may, undoubtedly, be increased in size, and, probably, improved in flavor. Like other Hickories, it does not transplant well, and must be removed from the seed-bed when one year old. It is said to be tardy in coming into bearing, though producing abundantly when well grown. This fault may, perhaps, be corrected by cultivation.

The nuts of the Pecan tree would be more abundant in the market but for the practice, worthy only of barbarians, of felling the trees, to come at the fruit more easily. This was extensively done along the Illinois river when I first settled in the west forty years since. It is said that the same vandalism is still perpetrated where it can be done with impunity.

If, on trial, it should be ascertained that the Pecan can be successfully grafted on the Black Walnut or Butternut, its growth would, probably, be more rapid, and, consequently, its propagation and improvement facilitated.

6. *Carya amara—Bitternut Hickory.*

Leaflets, seven to eleven; oblong lanceolate; serrate, smooth; fruit, globular with ridged or prominent seams opening half way down; nut, inversely heart-shaped; its shell thin.

The Bitternut usually grows in richer soil than most other species of Hickory. It is common in the Western States on rich bottom lands, and is abundant on the skirts of the prairies where the soil is deep and fertile; where it is accompanied by the Black Walnut, Red Elm, Laurel Oak and Bur Oak. It is a large tree, reaching the height of sixty or seventy feet. The wood is similar to that of other species of Hickory but is inferior in quality. In large old trees it is rather soft, and of less value than in younger trees for any purpose but fuel.

In some parts of Northern Illinois a small insect, the Scolytus Caryae, has for several years past been destroying the Bitternut. The perfect insect, a small black beetle, bores through the bark in the latter part of summer, and forms a vertical chamber, next the wood, usually about an inch long. On each side of this chamber the eggs are deposited from ten to twenty or thirty in number. When hatched the larvæ bore horizontally in opposite directions through the inner bark, forming parallel or slightly diverging tracks, separating the bark from the wood. The circulation of the sap is prevented and the tree consequently dies. The ravages of this insect commenced in the vicinity of Princeton, about fourteen years since, and appear likely to continue while any trees remain to operate upon.

The Bitternut Hickory is one of the least desirable species for propagation. The inferiority of its timber and its liability to destruction by insects are sufficient to discourage its culture.

Carya microcarpa, another species, grows in some parts of the Atlantic States, but I am unacquainted with it, and do not know that it is found in the Western country.

CASTANEA—CHESTNUT.

Natural Order, Cupuliferæ.

Sterile flowers clustered near the ends of the branches in long, naked cylindrical catkins; fertile flowers at the base of the sterile; two or three together in an ovoid, scaly, prickly involucre; nuts, coriaceous, ovoid, enclosed two or three together, or solitary in the hard coriaceous and very prickly involucre; cotyledons, very thick; somewhat plaited, cohering together; remaining underground in germination.

The Chestnut is found from Maine to Michigan and Kentucky, but is a stranger to the States of Wisconsin and Illinois; and I think has never been found west of the Mississippi. It is said most to abound in the mountainous districts from Virginia to Georgia, and in East Tennessee. I have seen it near the Yazoo river in alluvial lands. It seems to prefer the sides and neighborhood of hills and mountains, with a dry, sandy or gravelly soil. It will thrive on the dry prairies of Illinois, but does not appear to grow more rapidly in the richer soils than in poorer lands. It will grow in almost any soil except a wet one. As it is mostly found native on soils that are not very rich and are naturally well drained, it may well be doubted if it will succeed on the rich flat lands of Illinois and Iowa, where the subsoil is often, for great part of the year, saturated with stagnant water. In these States soils underlaid with sand or gravel — the banks of ravines — river bluffs, and uneven lands generally, will probably be found the most suitable places for planting it.

Wherever the soil is suitable, and the winters not too severe, few forest trees merit the attention of the grower more than the Chestnut. It is scarcely probable that it will endure the climate of Minnesota; perhaps not that of Northern Iowa; but where it will succeed it will amply repay cultivation. Its wood is largely employed in the manufacture of furniture, and for the inside finish of railroad cars and steam-boats. It is strong, elastic and durable; and, although coarse-grained, is, when oiled and varnished, very handsome. Its durability renders it particularly valuable for posts, which are made of small trees. Chestnut rails are said to last more than fifty years. As fuel it is not esteemed. The nuts usually bring from six to ten dollars per bushel in the market, and have even been sold for twelve dollars; so that an acre of well-grown Chestnut trees may be the source of considerable profit aside from the value of the timber. Trees fifteen years old are, commonly, large enough to produce a peck of fruit each, and eighty to a hundred trees of that age will grow on an acre without greatly interfering with each other. Lands utterly worthless for cultivation, may be made to yield an income by planting them with the Chestnut.

The nuts become larger by cultivation. The third generation has been grown in Illinois, and, after each successive planting, the nuts were increased in size. Dr. B. T. Long of Alton, has repeatedly exhibited Chestnut burrs from a tree of his own raising, each containing seven perfect nuts. This, he stated, was its customary, though not uniform, habit of production. The European variety produces larger fruit than the American, but it is less sweet and rich, and the tree is less hardy, not enduring the winters of Northern Illinois.

One great advantage belonging to the Chestnut over most other trees, is the facility with which it is renewed after being cut down. Sprouts spring up from the stumps and grow with astonishing rapidity; needing no other care than the exclusion of stock, and thinning where they are too numerous. In fifteen years this new growth will be large enough to cut a second time. In this way a grove may be reproduced for an indefinite period of time. The cutting should always be done in the winter.

As an ornamental tree in open ground, the Chestnut is one of the finest of trees, forming a round, spreading, or sometimes a conical head, and clothed with rich, glossy foliage. When full-grown, it is a large and long-lived tree. Michaux mentions trees which he measured in the forests of North Carolina, which, at six feet from the ground, were fifteen or sixteen feet in circumference, and equaled the loftiest trees in stature. Europe, however, boasts of the largest Chestnut trees. The Great Chestnut of Mount Etna, one hundred and sixty feet in circumference, is famous, and there are others near it of immense size. Michaux describes one growing near Sancerre, in France, one hundred and twenty miles from Paris, which, at six feet from the ground, is thirty feet in circumference. Six hundred years ago it was called the Great Chestnut; and, though it is believed to be more than one thousand years old, its trunk is still sound, and its branches annually laden with fruit.

When gathered for planting, Chestnuts must not be allowed to become dry, and care should be taken that they do not heat, which they are likely to do if piled together in any considerable quantity. They should be mixed with an equal bulk of sand, and kept through the winter in a cool place, where they will be damp, but not wet. If properly treated, very few will fail to vegetate. If sown where the trees are to remain, they may be placed one foot apart; if to be transplanted, which should be done in autumn, two or three inches will be sufficient. In case the young trees are to remain where planted, they should receive some protection the first winter. This may be done by ridging, as directed in the chapter on Propagation, and covering lightly with some kind of litter. After the first winter they need no protection. For planting, seed grown in the Northern States is to be preferred to that from more southern latitudes.

The Chestnut does not transplant well when more than five or six feet high, even if previously transplanted or root-pruned. When it is desirable to remove larger trees, it is best to cut them off at the surface of the ground immediately after planting, and allow sprouts to grow from the stump. In this way a finer tree may be obtained than from the original stem in case it survived, which would be a matter of great uncertainty. When planted for the production of fruit, the trees should be placed not less than fifteen or twenty feet apart. If it be an object to save seeds in planting for timber, they may be placed eight feet apart, and the intermediate spaces planted with corn or potatoes for two years, and afterwards filled with Silver Maple, or some other tree easily propagated, to be cut out as the Chestnuts increase in size.

Castanea pumila—Chincapin.

Leaves, oblong, acute, serrate, with pointed teeth; whitened, downy underneath; nut, solitary, not flattened.

The Chincapin, which is really the Chestnut on a smaller scale, is not found further north than Pennsylvania and New Jersey. Growing wild in these States, it is little more than a shrub, but becomes larger when cultivated. In the Southern States, it grows sometimes to the height of thirty feet or more. The fruit is sweet, but small; the wood still more durable than that of the Chestnut, but its dwarfish size will prevent its culture by any but amateurs. It is propagated like the Chestnut.

CATALPA.

Natural Order, Bignoniaceæ.

Calyx, two-parted; corolla, bell-shaped, swelling; the five-lobed, spreading border irregular and two-lipped; fertile, stamens two or sometimes four; the others sterile; pod long, cylindrical.

Catalpa bignonioides—Catalpa.

Leaves, heart-shaped, pointed, downy beneath; flowers, in open compound panicles.

The Catalpa grows in the Southwestern States, and appears to be indigenous in Southern Illinois and Indiana. It has long been cultivated as an ornamental tree further north. At Princeton, Illinois, in latitude 41° 30′, it is hardy. I have trees of my own planting two feet in diameter. In its native forests, it reaches the height of fifty or sixty feet, with a diameter of from eighteen to twenty-four inches. The leaves are large, the flowers showy, and when in bloom the tree is extremely beautiful. The weight of its foliage renders it somewhat liable to be broken by violent winds when growing in exposed situations. The leaves are rather tardy in appearing in spring, and are cast with the first frosts of autumn.

The Catalpa is easily naturalized where the winters are not too severe, young plants springing up readily from the scattered seeds of older trees. The wood is light, and takes a brilliant polish. It resembles that of the Butternut, but is more durable. Posts of the Catalpa, well seasoned when set, have been proved by experiment to be very lasting. In Southern Illinois it is used for that purpose in preference to any other timber. I have been assured by credible persons that posts are still in use that have stood for forty years without the appearance of decay. In thick forests in that region it reaches the height of eighty or ninety feet. Its cultivation, to a limited extent, may be recommended on account of its durability, the rapidity of its growth, and the ease with which it is raised from seed.

The seeds are contained in a long, slender pod; they are thin, flat, and enveloped in a long, narrow, membraneous wing. If sown in spring, and covered thinly, they vegetate readily, and the young trees transplant easily.

CELTIS—NETTLE TREE, HACKBERRY.

Natural Order, Urticaceæ.

Calyx, five or six parted, persistent; stamens, five or six; ovary, one-celled, with a single ovule; stigmas, two, long and pointed, recurved; fruit, a round berry; flowers, greenish, axillary.

Celtis occidentalis, var. crassifolia.—Hackberry.

Leaves, obliquely cordate, ovate, acuminate, serrate, thick, very rough.

The Hackberry is found in the Western States, almost exclusively upon the richest soils, in which it often attains the height of eighty feet, with a diameter of only eighteen or twenty inches, and a trunk straight and undivided to a great height. It is usually braced on all sides by large projecting roots, which rise two feet or more above the surface of the ground. The foliage and spray resemble those of the Elm, but the tree is less spreading. Its fruit is about the size of a pea, with a sweet pulp enveloping the seed, and is often produced in considerable quantity. Its wood is white, and splits easily, but speedily decays when exposed to the weather. Rails made from it last but a short time. It is sometimes sawed into lumber to be used for inside work, but it shrinks and swells greatly with the alternations of dryness and moisture in the atmosphere. Its most important use is for the manufacture of flat hoops for flour and fruit barrels, for which it is well fitted.

The Hackberry is a fine tree, but cannot be recommended for cultivation for the sake of its timber. The Nettle tree of the Eastern States, of which this is a variety, greatly resembles it. Another species, the Celtis Mississippiensis, is found in Southern Illinois, but I am unacquainted with it.

CERCIS—RED-BUD, JUDAS TREE.

Natural Order, Leguminosæ.

Calyx, five-toothed; corolla, imperfectly papilionaceous; standard smaller than the wings, and enclosed by them in the bud; the keel petals larger, and not united; stamens, ten, distinct, rather unequal; pod, oblong, flat, many-seeded, the upper suture with a winged margin; embryo, straight.

Cercis Canadensis—Red-bud.

Leaves, pointed; pods, nearly sessile above the calyx.

The Red-bud is common in the Western States, growing on the banks of streams, the sides of ravines, and river bluffs, and on the skirts of the prairies. It is a large shrub, or small tree, from fifteen to thirty feet high. It flowers early in spring, before the appearance of the leaves. The flowers are small, but very numerous, completely covering the twigs and small branches. When first open, they are of a bright red color, fading to a pale pink before falling. They are produced while the tree is quite small. Meehan mentions a specimen in the Bartram Garden, at Philadelphia, thirty-five feet high.

The Red-bud is easily raised from seed sown in the spring. The seed is commonly abundant, and is contained in small, flat pods. I have sometimes found the seed nearly all destroyed by an insect resembling the Peabug (Bruchus pisi), but much smaller.

Cercis siliquastrum.

The European Judas tree much resembles the American species, but is said to be inferior in beauty. I have never seen it in flower, as it is not hardy in Northern Illinois.

CHIONANTHUS.

Natural Order, Oleaceæ.

Calyx, four-parted, very small, persistent; corolla, of four long and linear petals, barely united at the base; stamens, two, rarely three or four, on the base of the corolla, very short; stigma, notched; berry, fleshy, globular, becoming one-celled and one-seeded.

Chionanthus Virginica—Fringe Tree.

Leaves, oval, oblong, or obovate, lanceolate, smoothish, or rather downy, veiny; berry, purple, with a bloom, ovoid.

This is a small tree, growing from twenty to thirty feet high, but flowering when only four or five feet high. It is native from Southern Pennsylvania southward, and is hardy much farther north. It is very ornamental when in bloom, the long, narrow petals resembling fringe cut from white paper, but it seldom continues in flower more than a week or ten days. It blossoms in June, and its dark purple berries grow in clusters. It thrives best in a moist soil. It is commonly propagated by seeds, but its growth is quite slow. It may be grafted on the Ash, and if this were done at standard height, a fine tree would be produced much sooner than in any other way. It may also be grown from layers, but does not root very readily. The seeds should be sown in a cool, shaded situation.

CLADRASTIS—YELLOWWOOD.

Natural Order, Leguminosæ.

Calyx, five-toothed; standard large, roundish, reflexed; the keel petals and wings straight, oblong; stamens, ten, distinct; filaments slender, incurved above; pod, linear, flat, thin, marginless; four to six-seeded; two-valved. Leaves, pinnate; leaflets, seven to eleven, oval or ovate; flowers in panicled racemes; white, showy.

Cladrastis tinctoria. Virgilia—Yellowwood.

The Virgilia is a middle-sized tree, rarely exceeding forty feet in height, and one foot in diameter. It is found in Kentucky and Tennessee, but is hardy several degrees further north. It is highly esteemed as an ornamental tree. The foliage is handsome, and he flowers numerous and showy. They are white, and produced in long, pendulous racemes. The wood is said to possess valuable qualities, but the rarity of. the tree precludes the idea of its cultivation for timber to any considerable extent. Its growth from seed is slow for the first three or four years, but is afterwards more rapid. The seed should be kept in moist sand through the winter. If sown dry in spring, it will not always vegetate till the next year.

CORNUS—CORNEL, DOGWOOD.

Natural Order, Cornaceæ.

Flowers, perfect (in some foreign species, diœcious); calyx, four-toothed; petals, four, oblong, spreading; stamens, four; filaments, slender; style, slender; stigma, slender, flat or capitate; berry, small, with a two-celled and two-seeded stone.

Cornus florida—Flowering Dogwood.

Leaves, ovate, pointed, acutish at the base; leaves of the involucre one and a-half inches long, inversely heart-shaped, or notched; fruit, oval.

This species of Cornus is the only one in the United States meriting the name of a tree. It is more or less common in most parts of the country south of latitude 43°, growing from fifteen to thirty-five feet high, the largest having a diameter of nine or ten inches. The wood is very hard, strong, heavy, and fine grained, and takes a brilliant polish. It is applied to various uses, for which wood of that description is needed.

The flowers are small, and collected in clusters, which are surrounded by a large involucre composed of four white leaves. These involucres are numerous enough to cover the tree with bloom, and render it one of the most showy and ornamental. The berries, which are red, are also conspicuous.

The seeds of the Dogwood do not vegetate till the second or third year. To make them grow the first year, Michaux gives the following method:—The seeds, in the fall, are cleared of their pulpy covering by rubbing them in water; they are then covered with earth in a box, and placed in the cellar till spring, care being taken to keep the earth moist.

DIOSPYROS—DATE PLUM, PERSIMMON.

Natural Order, Ebenaceæ.

Calyx and corolla, four to six-lobed; stamens, sixteen in the sterile flowers and eight in the fertile, in the latter imperfect; berry, large, with the calyx at the base; four to eight-seeded; flowers, diœciously polygamous.

Diospyros Virginiana—Persimmon.

Leaves, ovate, oblong, smooth; peduncles, very short; calyx, four-parted; corolla, between bell-shaped and urn-shaped; styles, four; two-lobed at the apex; ovary, eight-celled.

The Persimmon is commonly a small tree, although in favorable situations it grows to the height of from forty to sixty feet, with a diameter of eighteen to twenty-four inches. Trees of this size were formerly found near the mouth of the Illinois river. The leaves are from four to six inches long, of a fine, glossy green above and glaucous beneath. When the tree is grown by itself, the top is round, or conical, rather open, with crooked, twisted branches. The fruit varies in size, shape and time of ripening; when green, or not fully ripe, it is intensely astringent. The fruit is best if ripened before severe frosts occur. Freezing removes the astringency, but is not, as some suppose, necessary for complete ripening. If the fruit has not reached a certain stage of maturity before freezing, it is rendered worthless. The strong tendency of the Persimmon to the production of varieties, renders it highly probable that the fruit may be greatly improved by cultivation.

The wood of the Persimmon is hard, heavy, fine-grained, and elastic. It is proper for turning, and is said to be superior to Ash for the shafts of carriages; the scarcity of stocks of proper size alone preventing its common use for that purpose. As an ornamental tree, it is highly deserving notice. It is found on the Illinois river, in latitude 40°, and is hardy much farther north.

The seed may be sown in the fall, or kept moist till spring. The young plants should be removed from the seed-bed when one year old; they will not transplant well if allowed to remain longer, as they form a single tap-root descending deep into the earth.

FAGUS—BEECH.

Natural Order, Cupuliferæ.

Staminate flowers numerous, in globose, pedunculate, pendulous catkins; fertile flowers in pairs, on a short peduncle, in an ovoid, prickly involucre; pistil, with the base covered by the calyx; styles, three, awl-shaped; nut, triangular.

Fagus ferrugina—American Beech.

Leaves, oblong, ovate, taper-pointed, distinctly and often coarsely toothed; petioles and midrib soon nearly naked; prickles of the fruit recurved or spreading.

The Beech is one of the loftiest trees of the American forests, sometimes reaching the height of one hundred feet. It occupies a wide range of latitude, being found from Canada to the Gulf of Mexico, though in the latter locality it is found only occasionally in swamps. It is a stranger to the neighborhood of the prairies of Illinois and Iowa. It grows to the greatest size in deep, moist soils. The largest Beech I ever saw grew upon the banks of the Funegusha Creek, a small, rapid stream, emptying into the Yazoo River on the east side. As near as could be judged without actual measurement, it was not less than from twelve to fifteen feet in circumference. The roots of the Beech run near the surface of the soil, and often appear above it. If the trees are felled in winter, they send up a great number of sprouts, so that a Beech forest is easily renewed.

The wood of the Beech speedily decays when exposed to the alternations of dryness and moisture, but is durable when kept dry, and incorruptible when kept constantly under water. It is hard, fine-grained, and compact, and, when seasoned, does not warp. It is largely used for shoe lasts, plane stocks, and the handles of mechanics' tools generally. It is employed in the frame-work of buildings, and the saplings are used for hoops. As fuel, it is considered inferior to the Sugar Maple.

The nuts are triangular, growing in pairs in a tough, scaly husk. They are among the most delicious

American Ash.

of nuts, and in some seasons are produced abundantly, but they are so small that they are only collected in small quantities by children. In some parts of Europe, where they abound, they are largely gathered for the manufacture of oil.

The Beech cannot be recommended as one of the most profitable trees for forest culture, nevertheless, it is worthy the attention of those who may plant upon a large scale. It is a beautiful tree, and several varieties are cultivated for ornament. For propagation, the seed is treated like that of the Chestnut.

FRAXINUS—ASH.

Natural Order, Oleaceæ.

Flowers, polygamous or diœcious; calyx, four-cleft, or none; petals, four, wanting in American species; stamens, two, sometimes three or four; anthers, large; style, single; stigma, two-cleft; fruit, a one or two-celled samara or key, flattened, winged at the apex; one or two-seeded.

Among the timber trees of the United States, the Ashes occupy a position of primary importance, No other tree, except the Oak, is applied to such varied and important uses. It combines lightness, strength, and elasticity in so high a degree, that no other tree could be found fully to supply its place. Most of the different species of Ash greatly resemble each other in the quality of their wood, but the White and Blue are undoubtedly the best and most profitable for cultivation. Ash timber is extensively employed in the manufacture of farming tools. It is said that European farmers prefer agricultural implements of American manufacture to those of the same pattern made at home, on account of the excellence of the Ash timber used in their construction. The rapid consumption of Ash wood for this and other purposes must soon greatly enhance its price, and there is little room for doubt that the Ash will be found one of the most profitable trees that can be planted.

1. *Fraxinus Americana—White Ash.*

Branchlets and petioles, smooth; leaflets, seven to nine, ovate or lance-oblong, pointed, pale, smooth or pubescent underneath, somewhat toothed or entire; fruit, terete, and marginless below; above, extended into a lanceolate, oblanceolate, or wedge linear wing.

Among the American species of Ash, the White Ash is one of the most valuable and worthy of culture, for the qualities of its wood and the rapidity of its growth. When full grown, it is one of the largest trees of our forests. I well recollect trees in Western Massachusetts three feet in diameter, with a straight shaft free from branches to the height of forty feet or more, but such are no longer to be found in the thickly settled parts of the country. The largest Ash tree I ever met with was one near my native place, which was felled more than forty years since for the manufacture of scythe snathes. The trunk was five feet in diameter, and perfectly sound. The tree was not lofty, the top having been broken off by a tornado many years before.

The White Ash abounds in the Provinces of the Dominion, in most parts of New England, New York, and the Northern States generally, but is fast becoming scarce. It is common, but not abundant, in Northern Illinois and Iowa, and becomes less frequent in proceeding southward. A cold climate appears to suit it best. I have never met with very large trees of the Ash in the vicinity of the prairies of Illinois and Iowa, although the soil is well suited to its growth; but this may readily be accounted for from the fact that it is one of the trees most easily destroyed by the fires which annually ravaged these countries previous to their settlement. I have been informed that in Southern Kansas the White Ash is small, crooked, and worthless for any purpose except fuel.

The White Ash will not thrive in very poor, dry lands. A cool, deep, moist soil seems most congenial to its growth. The trees which have grown most rapidly afford the best timber; that taken from stunted, slow-growing trees, is comparatively weak and brittle. The prairie soils of Iowa and Northern and Central Illinois are well adapted to the growth of the White Ash. Other species would, perhaps, be of more value further south.

Besides its employment in the manufacture of agricultural implements, Ash timber is extensively used in the construction of carriages and furniture. It is esteemed for fire-wood. The supply is fast diminishing, and the demand increasing, and those who propose to engage in tree planting cannot be too soon in taking measures to meet it.

The American species of Ash are diœcious, that is, the fertile and barren flowers are on different trees. Seed is produced by White Ash trees which grow in open ground. The seed is ripe by the first of October, and falls with the first sharp frosts. If sown in the fall, it should be thinly covered with earth, and straw or litter laid over it to prevent it from being washed out by heavy rains. The litter must be taken off in spring. If to be sown in spring, it should be mixed with moderately damp sand. If kept dry through the winter, it is not likely to vegetate. The White Ash bears transplanting well, even when of considerable size. It is a handsome ornamental tree, and is rarely attacked by insects. The only exception I know of is the May-bug (Lachnostema fusca), which sometimes devours the leaves early in the summer.

2. *Fraxinus quadrangulata—Blue Ash.*

Branchlets, square, glabrous; leaflets, seven to nine, short-stalked, oblong, ovate, or lanceolate, pointed, sharply serrate, green both sides; fruit, narrowly-oblong, blunt, and of the same width at both ends, or slightly narrowed at the base.

The Blue Ash is not found in the Atlantic States, and in the valley of the Mississippi grows principally upon the river bottoms. It seems to prefer the richest soils. It is common on the waters of the Illinois river as far north as Bureau County, beyond which it becomes rare. It is a large tree, growing sixty or seventy feet high, with a diameter of two feet or more. It is easily distinguished from other species by the quadrangular shape of the young shoots. The bark on old trees is not like that of White Ash, deeply furrowed, and divided into small squares.

The wood of the Blue Ash is not inferior to that of any other species in the qualities which characterize the genus, and possesses one advantage over them all —that of greater durability when exposed to the alternations of dryness and moisture. This has been satisfactorily proved in its use for posts, stakes, and the rails of rural fences. In the regions where it grows, it is extensively employed for the same purposes as the White Ash. It was formerly much used for the flooring of houses. Michaux says that he was informed that a blue color could be extracted from the inner bark. If this be true, it is probably the origin of the name. As an ornamental tree, it is equal in beauty to any other species of the genus.

As the Blue Ash belongs naturally to a more southern climate than the White Ash, its cultivation may be recommended in preference to the latter, south of latitude 40. It may probably be successfully planted further north than its native localities where the soil is fertile. It is propagated in the same manner as the White Ash.

3. *Fraxinus sambucifolia—Black Ash.*

Branchlets and petioles, glabrous; leaflets, seven to eleven, sessile, oblong-lanceolate, tapering to a point, serrate, obtuse or rounded at the base, green and smooth both sides; fruit, linear, oblong, or narrow elliptical, blunt at both ends.

The Black Ash is sometimes sixty or seventy feet high, and two feet in diameter. It is found in the same latitudes as the White Ash, but commonly grows in a wetter soil; hence it is often called Swamp Ash and Water Ash. It will, nevertheless, thrive in soils that suit the White Ash. The wood is more elastic than that of any other species. It divides easily into thin, narrow strips, which are used for making baskets and hoops for flour, salt, and fruit barrels. For the latter purpose, it is the most economical wood that can be procured, and it is, perhaps, the most important use to which the Black Ash is applied. It is less durable than other species of Ash when exposed to the changes of dryness and moisture. It makes good fuel when dry, but when green can scarcely be burned at all. The ashes are extremely rich in alkali.

The Black Ash may be recommended for planting on grounds that are too wet to produce other valuable kinds of timber. Its uses are important, though less varied than those of other species of Ash. Propagation same as the preceding species.

4. *Fraxinus pubescens*—*Red Ash.*

Branchlets and petioles, velvety-pubescent; leaflets, seven or nine, ovate, or oblong-lanceolate, taper-pointed, almost entire, pale, or more or less pubescent beneath; fruit ovate at the base, flattish, and two-edged, the edges gradually dilated into the long oblanceolate or linear-lanceolate wing.

The Red Ash is said to be more multiplied than any other species in Pennsylvania, New Jersey, Maryland and Virginia. According to Dr. Gray, it is rare west of the Alleghanies. It is found in various localities in Illinois and Iowa, but I have not found it in the vicinity where I reside, and am not intimately acquainted with it.

The Red Ash grows on the banks of rivers, and in most rich soils, similar to those preferred by the White Ash. It is a smaller tree than the White Ash, and, if the testimony of Michaux may be believed, is of much less rapid growth. The wood is employed for the same purposes as the White Ash and Blue Ash, and possesses all the properties for which they are esteemed. Although inferior in size to the White Ash, this species may probably be found suited to cultivation in warmer climates than the former. It is propagated in the same manner as other species.

5. *Fraxinus viridis*—*Green Ash.*

Smooth throughout; leaflets, five to nine, ovate or oblong-lanceolate, often wedge-shaped at the base and serrate above; bright green both sides; fruit, ovate at the base, striated, two-edged or margined, gradually dilated into a wing like that of the Red Ash.

This species, which does not rank above a middle-sized tree, is found mostly upon the banks of rivers, and is common in the Western States. It is a very handsome tree, with bright-green, glossy leaves, which are nearly alike on both sides. The wood possesses the same properties which distinguish other species of Ash. It is of vigorous and rapid growth, and nothing but its smaller size renders it less eligible for culture than the preceding. It is propagated like the rest. The seed germinates readily if sown dry in spring—that of the White and Blue Ash will not.

6. *Fraxinus excelsior—European Ash.*

Leaflets, subsessile, oblong-lanceolate, alternate, serrate; flowers, without petals; sèeds, emarginate at the apex.

The European Ash is a large and lofty tree, growing in situations analogous to those in which the White Ash and Red Ash are found in America. Several varieties are cultivated in the United States for ornament. It is propagated in European nurseries for forest planting, and is considered one of the most valuable kinds of timber. It is, nevertheless, confessedly inferior to the White Ash and Blue Ash in the very qualities for which it is most valued; there is, therefore, no reason for recommending it for forest culture in America.

Another species of Ash of small size, F. platycarpa—the Carolina Water Ash—is found in swamps in the Southern States, but does not appear to merit notice as a forest tree.

GLEDITSCHIA—HONEY LOCUST.

Natural Order, Leguminosæ.

Flowers, polygamous; calyx, of three to five spreading sepals, united at the base; petals, as many as the sepals and equaling them, the two lower sometimes united; stamens, as many, distinct, inserted with the petals on the base of the calyx; pod, flat, many-seeded.

1. *Gleditschia triacanthos—Honey Locust, Three-thorned Acacia.*

Thorns, stout, often triple or compound, frequently wanting; leaflets, lanceolate-oblong, somewhat serrate; pods, linear, elongated, often twisted.

The Honey Locust appears to be much more common west of the Alleghanies than in the Atlantic States. In the State of Illinois it is found principally upon the river bottoms, but frequently occurs on rich uplands. It sometimes towers to the height of eighty or one hundred feet, with a diameter of three or four feet. The general appearance of the tree is distinct from all others, and never fails to attract notice. The leaves are pinnate; the leaflets smald and of a deep green hue. It has been much plantet, for ornament, and is quite graceful, but its foliage is too thin to afford much shade. The pods, when ripe, contain a sweet pulp, and are eaten by domestic animals, but seem scarcely so well suited to the human stomach as to justify the conclusion of the Hardshell preacher, that they constituted the food of John-the-Baptist.

The Honey Locust affords excellent fuel, and the wood is extremely hard when seasoned, but its character as a valuable timber tree does not appear to be well established. Michaux speaks disparagingly of its qualities, while others assert that it is very durable. It only occurs occasionally in the forests of Northern Illinois, consequently its use has never attracted much attention. It is sometimes split into rails, and is employed for the hubs and felloes of wagon wheels. I have seen it used for posts, but too recently to afford evidence of its durability for that purpose.

This tree has of late been highly recommended as a hedge plant, and is to some extent propagated for that object. The idea is not new. It was extolled many years since, and more than forty years ago I saw it planted for hedges in Massachusetts, but for some reason the practice was not continued. I have never seen a Honey Locust hedge of long standing, and cannot give an opinion in regard to its merits.

Most of the Honey Locust trees which I have met with in Northern Illinois were destitute of thorns. In some parts of the country they are nearly or quite all armed with them. This fact would seem to indicate the proper way of selecting seed for the different objects in planting. Seed for hedge plants should be gathered from thorny trees; that for ornamental or timber trees from such as are unarmed. The seed of thornless trees will commonly, though not uniformly, produce thornless plants, and it is presumable that seeds from thorny trees will follow the same rule. The idea advanced by some, that clipping will develop thorns upon thornless plants, seems to have its foundation in fancy rather than in fact. The armature of the Honey Locust, however desirable in a hedge plant, is a nuisance in an ornamental or timber tree. Some of the trees bristle with thorns to such a degree that not even a squirrel can ascend them. The clippings from hedges should be gathered up and burned, since the thorns are not only likely to pierce the feet of animals, but are strong and sharp enough to penetrate the upper leather of the boots or shoes of the unlucky individual who may chance to tread on them.

The Honey Locust is diœcious, the greater part of the trees producing no seed. Young trees are easily raised by sowing the seed in the fall or spring. Some recommend scalding the seed before sowing. I have never found this necessary, and have known it to be destroyed by so doing.

2. *Gleditschia monosperma—Water Locust.*

Thorns, slender, mostly simple; leaflets, ovate or oblong; pods oval and seeded, without pulp.

The Water Locust is a smaller tree than the Honey Locust, which it greatly resembles. It is found in Southern Illinois, and southward, growing principally in the swamps which border the rivers. It grows to the height of fifty or sixty feet. Its wood is inferior to that of the preceding species, and is seldom used where it is most common.

GYMNOCLADUS—KENTUCKY COFFEE TREE.

Flowers, diœcious, regular; calyx, tubular below; five-cleft; petals, five, oblong, equal, inserted on the summit of the calyx tube; stamens, ten, distinct, short, inserted with the petals; pod, oblong, flattened, hard, pulpy inside; several seeded.

Gymnocladus Canadensis, is the only species of this genus growing in the United States—I think, the only one known. It is found from Canada and Western New York to Louisiana, and grows only in the richest lands. It is a lofty tree, but slender in proportion to its height. The leaves are doubly pinnate, two or three feet in length. It is a very beautiful tree, and is cultivated in the Atlantic States for ornament. Its appearance in winter is peculiar, from the fewness of its branches and the large size of its terminal shoots—which is, perhaps, the origin of its French name, *Chicot,* Stump Tree.

The wood of the Coffee Tree is of a rosy color; it is fine grained, compact, strong and durable. It is very suitable for cabinet work, and is esteemed for building. Its use, however, is very limited, on account of its scarcity in the greater part of the countries where it is native. The timber, even of young trees, contains a very small proportion of sap wood. It is of rapid growth, and its valuable properties recommend it for forest culture in suitable situations. A deep, rich soil is requisite to insure its full development.

The barren and fertile flowers are produced on different trees. The seeds are large, growing in a large

The Black Walnut.

curved pod, which remains on the tree till spring. The tree takes its name from the use of its seeds as a substitute for coffee. For propagation, they are sown early in spring. Cuttings of the roots are also used for this purpose. They are cut two or three inches long, and placed in boxes of earth, with the larger end near the surface, and very early in spring the boxes are placed in bottom heat in a propagating house or hot bed. When rooted, they are planted in open ground.

HALESIA—SNOW DROP TREE, SILVER BELL.

Natural Order, Styracaceæ.

Calyx, four-toothed, superior; corolla, four-cleft, twisted to the left; nut, winged, two-seeded.

Halesia tetraptera—Silver Bell.

Leaves, oblong-ovate; fruit, four-winged.

The Silver Bell is found in the upper part of Virginia, on the banks of the Ohio, and southward. It sometimes grows to the height of forty or fifty feet, but is usually smaller. It is valued only as an ornamental tree, for which purpose it is one of the most desirable. It produces a profusion of its white, bell-shaped flowers, even when quite small. It is hardy in Illinois as far north as latitude 42°, and probably beyond. The seed is contained in a four-winged capsule, very hard and bony. It may be sown in the fall, or kept moist till spring, but will not always germinate till the second year. I have usually found the seed from small plants worthless.

1. JUGLANS—WALNUT.

Natural Order, Juglandaceæ.

Sterile flowers, in simple catkins; calyx, three to six-cleft; fertile flowers, solitary, or several together on a peduncle, at the end of the branches; calyx, four-toothed; petals, four; fruit, with a fibrous, fleshy covering, and a mostly rough, irregularly furrowed nut-shell.

Juglans cinerea—Butternut.

Leaflets, oblong-lanceolate, pointed, rounded at the base, downy, especially underneath; the petioles and branchlets downy, with clammy hairs; fruit, oblong, clammy, pointed, the nut deeply sculptured, and rough with ragged ridges.

The Butternut is common throughout the northern half of the United States, east of the Rocky Mountains, and seems to attain its greatest development in cold climates. I have seen larger Butternut trees in New England than I ever met with in the Valley of the Mississippi. In the Western States it is found principally on the river bottoms. It seldom exceeds fifty or sixty feet in height, and two or three feet in diameter. When grown in open ground, the trunk branches at a small height, and forms a wide-spreading head. The wood is of a light brown color, fine grained, rather soft, and easily worked. Although less valuable than the Black Walnut, its uses are sufficiently varied and important to render its cultivation an object of consequence. It is easily raised from the seed, and grows rapidly. As a fruit-bearing tree it is not to be despised, The nuts are liked by most people, and it is extremely probable that they might, in no long period of time, be so far improved by cultivation as to become a market fruit. I have ascertained that a considerable improvement takes place from a single planting. The shell becomes thinner, the kernel larger, and of easier extraction. The European Walnut, in its primitive state, is said to be inferior to this in size and quality. The Butternut is propagated in the same manner as the Black Walnut.

2. *Juglans nigra—Black Walnut.*

Leaves, ovate-lanceolate, taper-pointed, somewhat heart-shaped, or unequal at the base, smooth above, the lower surface and the petioles minutely downy; fruit, spherical, roughly dotted; the nut corrugated.

The Black Walnut is found in the Atlantic States, but is far less multiplied than in the Valley of the Mississippi. It grows on the river bottoms, and on the uplands wherever the soil is deep and fertile. In the State of Illinois, next to the Oaks and Hickories, it is one of the most common trees. The majestic trees of this kind which once adorned the Illinois forests, have, however, mostly disappeared, and Black Walnut timber is now scarce where it was formerly most abundant.

The growth of the Black Walnut is quite rapid, and when fully developed, it becomes one of the largest forest trees. Thirty-five years since, specimens were frequent along the Bureau river, three to four feet in diameter, with trunks undivided from thirty to fifty feet. The largest Black Walnut I ever met with is one growing near Roslyn, on Long Island, about twenty miles from the city of New York. It stands on the grounds of William C. Bryant, and sprang from the seed in the year 1713, in the garden of a Quaker named Mudge. At three feet from the ground it is twenty-five feet in circumference. At the height of twelve or fifteen feet, the trunk divides into several branches, each of which, by itself, would constitute a large tree—the whole forming an immense canopy, overshadowing an area one hundred and fifty feet in diameter.

The valuable properties of the wood of the Black Walnut are well-known, and need not be enlarged upon here. The demand for the manufacture of gun stocks, for cabinet-work, and for the inside finish of houses, is very great, and the supply is fast becoming scarce. Taking into account the ease with which it is propagated, its rapid growth, the value of its timber, and the certainty that the demand can only cease with the supply, it would appear that hardly any other tree can be named more likely to repay the cost of planting and culture, wherever a suitable soil can be had.

The fruit of the Black Walnut is often produced abundantly before the trees have attained a large size. The nuts, when gathered for planting, should be laid in heaps on dry ground, and covered with straw or sods, with sufficient earth over all to exclude water, and prevent frequent thawing and freezing.

In spring, they may be planted in ground marked out in rows, four feet apart. The Black Walnut is inclined to throw out heavy side branches, and form a low, spreading top. It must, therefore, be thickly grown to produce tall timber. If seed be scarce, or if it is an object to make it go as far as possible, plant nuts eight feet apart in every other row, and plant the intermediate rows and spaces with corn or potatoes. After two years, the Walnuts will be well-established; the spaces should then be filled with Silver Maples, slips of White Willow, or some other fast-growing tree, easily and cheaply obtained, placed two feet apart. These are to be thinned out as occasion requires. The Black Walnut trees, at eight feet apart, will grow to such a size as to be of value for many purposes; but before becoming large enough for saw-logs, they must be thinned to two or three times that distance. Some attention should be given to pruning the young trees while small. The leading shoot will sometimes fork, or a side shoot of too vigorous growth be thrown out. These should be shortened, or cut out entirely.

The Black Walnut is a bad neighbor to many other trees, and should, as far as possible, be grown by itself. It is unfit for a screen to an orchard. Apple trees will not live long in its neighborhood, and the same is probably true of some, if not all, other fruit trees.

Some persons have thought it necessary to crack the nuts before planting them. This is altogether needless, even if it were not true that it is scarcely possible to do it without damaging the kernel so much as to prevent its germination. The nuts are sweet, but have a peculiar flavor, which is relished by some and very disagreeable to others. Varieties sometimes occur of superior flavor, which would seem to indicate that the fruit is capable of improvement.

3. *Juglans regia—English Walnut.*

Leaflets, five to nine, oval, glabrous, obscurely-serrate; fruit, oval, upon a short peduncle.

The English Walnut is a large tree, and is much cultivated in Europe, both for its fruit and its timber. Its fruit is largely imported, and sold in all parts of the country. As a timber tree, it is inferior to the Black Walnut—as an ornamental tree, to both that and the Butternut; yet it merits cultivation for the sake of its fruit, wherever the climate is not too severe. The tree is not hardy in Northern Illinois, and it is doubtful if it would succeed in the central parts of the State. Probably it might do well in the latitude of St. Louis. There are trees near the city of New York which bear fruit, but in the interior the blossoms are often destroyed by spring frosts, in latitudes where the tree withstands the winters. The best varieties are propagated by grafting. Like the Black Walnut, its neighborhood is said to be injurious to other trees, and the exhalations from it are so powerful as to affect disagreeably those who sleep in its shade.

KOELREUTERIA.

Natural Order, Sapindaceæ.

Calyx, five-parted; petals, four, each with two scales at the base; capsule, inflated, three-celled; leaves, alternate, pinnate; leaflets, ovate, coarsely-toothed; flowers, yellow, in panicles.

Koelreuteria paniculata—Koelreuteria.

This tree is a native of China, and is the only species known. It never exceeds the middle size, sometimes reaching the height of forty feet or more, but commonly of smaller stature. Its large, compound leaves, and large panicles of yellow flowers, which are produced in abundance in July and August, render it highly ornamental, and deserving a place in every collection of trees. It is quite hardy in most of the Northern States. In the rich soils of Northern Illinois, the young wood on small trees is occasionally injured in consequence of immature growth. This rarely, if ever, occurs after they have reached the height of ten or twelve feet, the shoots being then shorter, and the wood ripening better.

The wood of the Koelreuteria is hard, and fine-grained, but as the tree is not common, and has hitherto been cultivated for ornament only, nothing is known in regard to its utility in the arts. The seeds are produced in large, inflated capsules, and readily germinate when sown in spring. The tree may also be propagated by layers and cuttings of the roots.

LIQUIDAMBAR.

Natural Order, Hamamelaceæ.

Male flower, with common, four-leaved calyx, without a corolla; female calyx in a globe, four-leaved, without a corolla; styles, two; capsules many, in a globe, two-valved; seeds many, but only one or two perfecting.

Liquidambar styraciflua—Sweet Gum, Bilsted.

Leaves, rounded, deeply five to seven-lobed, smooth and shining, glandular, serrate, the lobes pointed.

In the States of the sea board, the Sweet Gum is found from Massachusetts to Mexico. West of the Alleghanies, it grows along the Ohio river and its tributaries, and in Southern Illinois, which appears to be its northern limit in the Mississippi valley. I have never met with it in the neighborhood of the prairies.

The Sweet Gum is a large and beautiful tree, with singular, star-like leaves, which become red in the fall, and add to the brilliant coloring of the woods at that season. The wood is compact and fine-grained, but not durable. It is applied to various uses where the tree is common, but there are so many other trees, of easier cultivation and of greater value, that it cannot be recommended for general culture. It is a fine ornamental tree, and merits the notice of the amateur for his arboretum, and of the planter on an extensive scale for the sake of variety.

The seeds are contained in a globular, woody fruit, studded with points. They are small, blackish, and furnished with a wing. They may be sown in autumn in loose soil, and protected by a covering of leaves or straw.

LIRIODENDRON—TULIP TREE.

Natural Order, Magnoliaceæ.

Sepals, three, reflexed; corolla, bell-shaped, six petalled; anthers, linear; pistils, flat, long, and narrow; carpels, one or two-seeded, disposed in spikes, deciduous, drawn out into a wing at the apex.

Liriodendron tulipifera—Tulip Tree, White Wood.

This tree is the only species of its genus, and it is a most magnificent one. It sometimes reaches the height of one hundred and forty feet, with a diameter of eight or nine feet, and, excepting the Sycamore or Buttonwood, is the largest and loftiest deciduous tree of the American forests. The name of Poplar or Yellow Poplar, by which it is called in many parts of the United States, is altogether misapplied, since it has no resemblance to, nor relationship with, the the Poplar family.

The Tulip Tree is found from New England to the Gulf of Mexico. It is multiplied in the Western States where the climate is not too severe, the soil deep and fertile, and the country mostly originally covered with forests. It is common in a large portion of Michigan, and in Southern Illinois; but although the soil and climate appear suited to its growth, it is a stranger to the prairie regions of Illinois and Iowa, probably for the reason that it was unable to withstand the fires that annually swept over these countries before their settlement.

The wood of the Tulip Tree is easily wrought, and ranks next to the White Pine for most uses to which that wood is applied. It is stronger and more durable than Pine, and is therefore better for some purposes. The best timber is grown upon a deep, rich, loam. Upon dry, gravelly soils, the wood is of inferior quality.

For ornamental purposes, this tree is equalled by few. Its leaves are large, singular in form, and of a bright, glossy green; the flowers are large, handsome, and of agreeable odor. They appear in great abundance on detached trees that are ten or twelve inches in diameter, and, in combination with the rich foliage, produce a fine effect. The trees will thrive in groves, or in clumps mingled with other trees, but produce the best effect standing singly. It is unfit for a street tree—it will not endure coal smoke, nor flourish in the atmosphere of cities and crowded villages. Except when small, it does not transplant well, unless it has been previously removed, or root-pruned once every two or three years.

The seeds are winged and clustered together, sixty or seventy in number, in the form of a cone, which falls apart late in autumn, or in winter. The seed produced by young trees is generally worthless. On large trees, that from the upper branches is considered the best; but even of this a large part is commonly abortive. The seed may be sown in the fall, or mixed with sand and kept till spring. If the young plants are to be removed, they should not be allowed to remain more than two years in the seed-bed.

As the Tulip Tree is not valuable for timber until it attains a considerable size, it is best, in planting for that purpose, to treat it as recommended in the case of the Black Walnut—place the plants eight feet apart, and fill the intermediate spaces with some inferior tree, to be cut out at the proper time. When this is done, the Tulip Tree should have two years the start, some cultivated crop, corn, beans, or potatoes being planted among them for that time.

Although the Tulip Tree will not make so speedy a return as some other trees for the outlay in planting and culture, yet it occupies a prominent place in the list of trees meriting extensive cultivation.

MACLURA.

Natural Order, Urticaceæ.

Male flowers, in a very short, nearly sessile panicle of about twelve flowers; female flowers, in close heads, on a short peduncle.

Maclura aurantiaca—Osage Orange, Bow-wood.

Leaves, ovate-acuminate, of a deep, shining green; male plant, with smaller leaves; fruit, large, golden-yellow, warty.

It is not intended here to discuss the merits of the Osage Orange as a hedge plant, nor to describe its treatment for that purpose. These have been abundantly set forth in other publications, and are pretty well understood where it is successfully grown. It is introduced to invite attention to the valuable qualities of its wood.

In rich bottom lands in Texas and Arkansas, the Osage Orange grows to the height of sixty feet. Probably it may never attain that size in more northern climates, but it will become large enough to be of great value. The wood is very hard, strong, elastic, and fine grained, and is nearly or quite incorruptible. I have been assured by persons who have resided where it is native, that, though it will waste away by the action of the weather, a rotten stick is never met with. It is said to be eminently fitted for the construction of carriage wheels, as when well-seasoned, it will not swell and shrink with the changes of moisture and dryness. I have used small trees for grape stakes, and found them very durable, and it is doubtless one of the best kinds of timber for posts. The plants are sold at cheap rates, and an acre or two planted for timber would be a good investment on any farm. The trees should be thickly grown—two feet apart in the rows, and kept trimmed to a single straight stem. The disposition it shows to sucker from the stump renders it probable that, like the Chestnut, a plantation would reproduce itself when cut down.

On account of its elasticity, the Osage Orange is used by the southern Indians for bows. The early French settlers called it Bois d'Arc, Bow-wood—a better name, it would seem, than Osage Orange.

MAGNOLIA.

Natural Order, Magnoliaceæ.

Sepals, three; petals, six to nine; stamens, numerous; pistils, numerous; carpels, disposed compactly in spikes, opening by the external angle; one or two-seeded, permanent; seeds, berry-like, hanging by an extensile thread.

The Magnolias comprise a considerable number of species, all of which are more or less desirable as ornamental trees, but of little value for timber. With one or two exceptions, their wood is seldom used for any purpose whatever. The bark of some species is sometimes employed as a substitute for Peruvian bark. They all produce their blossoms while young.

1. *Magnolia acuminata—Cucumber Tree.*

Leaves, oblong, pointed, green, and a little pubescent beneath; petals, glacous, green, tinged with yellow, oblong; cone of fruit, small, cylindrical.

The Cucumber Tree is found from Western New York, through Ohio and Indiana, to Southern Illinois, and southward. Excepting the Big Laurel of the Southern States, this is the largest of its genus, growing to the height of from sixty to ninety feet. It is quite hardy considerably further north than its native localities. In good soils it grows rapidly, and its fine shape, and the size and beauty of its foliage, render it a desirable ornamental tree. Unlike others of its genus, the flowers of this species, though large, add nothing to its beauty. They consist of six-twisted, straggling petals, without beauty either of form or color. The figure in Michaux's "*Sylva*," must have been taken by mistake from some other species, since neither in form nor color does it at all resemble the flower of the Cucumber Tree.

The wood resembles that of the Tulip Tree, but is less strong and durable. It is sawed into boards and used for the inside finish of houses, and for other purposes to which the Linden or Basswood is applied. It does not rank high among useful trees.

The seeds have a thin, pulpy covering, of a bright red color, and after leaving the cells of the cone in which they grow, remain awhile suspended by a white filament. They must be sown immediately, or kept in damp sand till spring, secure from mice. If allowed to become dry they will not vegetate. They are somewhat tardy in germinating after being sown. The young plants must be shaded from the hot sun while tender, and should be protected during the first winter. The tree may be propagated by layers, but the plants so produced are inferior to those raised from seed.

2. *Magnolia cordata*—*Yellow Cucumber Tree.*

Leaves, heart-shaped, somewhat ovate-acute, under surface woolly, upper surface smooth; petals, six or nine; flowers yellow.

This species, which is found in Georgia and South Carolina, grows to the height of forty or fifty feet. It is esteemed for the beauty of its yellow flowers, which form a fine contrast with the rich foliage. It is one of the most ornamental species, and it is probably nearly or quite as hardy as the preceding species, since it withstands the winters of Massachusetts. The wood is similar to that of the cucumber tree, but is seldom used, as the trees are not very common, even in their native localities.

Magnolia macrophylla—Great-leaved Magnolia.

Leaves, obovate-oblong, cordate at the narrowed base, pubescent and white beneath; petals, white, with a purple spot inside at the base; ovate; cone of the fruit, ovoid.

This species is not very common anywhere. It is found in the southeast part of Kentucky and in some other places in the Southern States. It is the most remarkable of the Magnolias for the size of its leaves and flowers. The leaves are from two to three feet long; the flowers nine or ten inches across. The tree is of moderate size and the wood of little value. It is of uncertain hardihood north of Philadelphia. It requires a well sheltered situation, as, on account of its heavy foliage, it is liable to be injured by high winds.

Magnolia glauca—Small Magnolia, Sweet Bay.

Leaves, oblong or oval, obtuse, white beneath; petals, white, rounded, obovate; cone of fruit, small, oblong.

The Small Magnolia grows near the sea coast from Massachusetts to Louisiana, but is seldom found far in the interior, and appears to be a stranger to the countries west of the Alleghanies. In the Southern States it grows to the height of thirty feet or more; about Philadelphia and New York it is of smaller size, and blooms when not more than five or six feet high. It is one of the most highly esteemed among the Magnolias for ornamental purposes. The leaves are of a dark shining green above, and nearly white beneath; in the far South they are evergreen. The flowers are two or three inches across; they are pure white, and most delightfully fragrant. Although found almost exclusively in swamps, it thrives in good upland soils, even better than in its native localities.

The seeds of the Small Magnolia soon become rancid. When gathered, they should immediately be placed in damp sand or rotten wood, and kept cool until they are sown. The young plants do not speedily appear; when up, they must be partially shaded from the sun. The tree appears to be hardy in Northern Illinois; but should be placed in a sheltered situation, and partially shaded.

Magnolia umbrella — Umbrella Tree.

Leaves, obovate-lanceolate, pointed at both ends, soon glabrous; petals, obovate-oblong.

The Umbrella Tree is found in Western New York, and thence southward, principally along the Alleghany mountains. It is only found in shaded situations, where the soil is deep, cool and rich. The finest specimens I have ever seen, grew on the banks of Black creek, a branch of the Yazoo river. The tree rarely exceeds the height of thirty feet. On vigorous trees, and in favorable situations, the leaves are often two feet long. They are disposed in a circle at the extremities of the branches; hence the name of Umbrella Tree. The flowers are large and beautiful, from six to eight inches broad; they are pure white, and have a sweet but heavy and not altogether agreeable odor.

I have not found the cultivation of this species satisfactory in Northern Illinois. The terminal buds are often injured by cold, and it has a persistent disposition to throw up new stems from the base, the old ones dying down; so that it never becomes a good sized shrub. It seems to require a sheltered, shady situation. In exposed localities the foliage becomes disfigured, being scorched by the sun and beaten by violent winds. Propagation same as the preceding.

Magnolia fraseri—Ear-leaved Umbrella Tree.

Leaves, oblong-obovate or spatulate, auriculate at the base, glabrous; petals, obovate-spatulate with narrow claws.

This species is found only along the Alleghany mountains in the Southern States, and is said not to be plentiful, even in its native localities. It grows to the height of forty feet, and is distinguished for the beauty of its foliage and flowers. It is preferred to the preceding species by cultivators, as the flowers have a pleasant fragrance; but it is not very common, and I am but slightly acquainted with it. It is hardy in the neighborhood of Philadelphia, and probably still further north.

Magnolia conspicua—Yulan.

Leaves, obovate, abruptly terminating in a point. This is a foreign species of great beauty, the flowers, which are white and fragrant, appearing in profusion before the leaves. It has not been yet tested in Northern Illinois. It is hardy about New York city, and is highly desirable where it will succeed. It grows to the height of twenty or thirty feet.

M. Soulangeana, according to Loudon, is a hybrid, between this species and M. purpurea; but Meehan says, between M. acuminata and M. purpurea. It can scarcely be called a tree, but is a magnificent shrub, flowering profusely in spring, and sometimes a second time in summer. The flowers are white, tinged with purple. It deserves a place in every garden where the climate is not too cold. As far as tested, it appears likely to be hardy in Northern Illinois.

M. purpurea is a Chinese species—a mere shrub, and not hardy in the Northern States. M. grandiflora, the evergreen Magnolia of the Southern States, is the finest species of the genus, but will not succeed at the North.

MORUS—MULBERRY.

Natural Order—Urticaceæ.

Flowers, monœcious or diœcious; male flowers in loose spikes without a corolla; female flowers in dense spikes; stamens, 4; stigmas, 2; calyx becoming a berry, each bearing one seed.

Morus rubra—Red Mulberry.

Leaves, heart-ovate, serrate, rough above, downy beneath, pointed, on young shoots often lobed; flowers often diœcious; fruit, dark purple.

The Red Mulberry is found throughout the greater part of the United States east of the Mississippi, and in some of the States west of that river. It sometimes grows to the height of sixty or seventy feet, but is commonly of smaller dimensions. It grows rapidly while young, but more slowly when a few inches in diameter. It is a handsome ornamental tree, and its fruit, which is quite palatable, is produced abundantly by most trees, although some are sterile. It merits notice, however, principally on account of its timber, which is strong, compact and singularly durable. It is esteemed by many fully equal to the Locust. It has been known to last fifty or sixty years when used for posts.

The fruit, which is increased in size by cultivation, ripens in June and July. To obtain the seed, it should be washed from the berries when fully ripe, and laid by till spring. The seed which floats in the water is worthless. It should be thinly covered when sown. Under favorable circumstances, the young plants will grow to the height of a foot or more the first year. The fruit ripens in succession for a considerable time, and drops when fully ripe, so that no considerable quantity can be obtained from a tree at once. Birds, too, are fond of the berries, and sometimes devour them as fast as they ripen.

Morus nigra—Black Mulberry.

Leaves, cordate, rough, small.

This species is a native ot Europe, and is cultivated there for its fruit, and also in some parts of the United States. It is a small tree, not hardy in the most northern States. Its growth is slow, and its wood not valuable. Michaux says the fruit is three or four times as large as that of the Red Mulberry. Meehan, on the other hand, avers that it is smaller. Having never seen the tree in fruit, I cannot decide the question.

Morus alba—White Mulberry.

Leaves, obliquely heart-ovate, acute, serrate, sometimes lobed, smooth and shining; fruit, whitish.

The White Mulberry is found in many parts of the United States. It was introduced from Europe for feeding silk worms, and is of little value for any other purpose. It grows to the height of twenty or thirty feet.

NYSSA—TUPELO.

Natural Order, Cornaceæ

Calyx of staminate flowers, five-parted, without a corolla; stamens, five to ten; pistillate flowers, five-stamened; fruit, a one-seeded drupe; nut oval, striated.

Nyssa multiflora—Black Gum, Tupelo, Pepperidge.

Leaves, oval, or obovate, commonly acuminate, glabrous, or villous pubescent when young, shining above, when old; fertile flowers, three to eight; fruit, ovoid, bluish black.

The Black Gum is a middle sized tree, and is found from Massachusetts to Illinois, and southward. It grows both in wet and dry soils. The fibres of the wood are so interwoven that it is almost impossible to split it; hence it is used for wagon hubs, rollers and cylinders. It is held in some estimation for ornamental purposes. Meehan says it is indispensable. It is difficult to transplant unless often removed, or root-pruned in the nursery. It is raised from seed, which commonly remains in the ground a year before vegetating.

Nyssa uniflora—Large Tupelo.

Leaves, oblong or ovate, entire or angular-toothed, long petioled; fertile flowers, solitary on a slender peduncle; fruit, oblong, blue.

This species is found only in the Southern States, where it often grows in water three or four feet deep. It is a large tree, with very soft, spongy wood, which is only used to make bowls and trays. The wood of the roots is sometimes used for corks. It is a handsome ornamental tree.

OSTRYA.

Natural Order, Cupuliferæ.

Sterile flowers in catkins of about twelve stamens in the axil of a scale-like bract, filaments somewhat united; fertile flowers in a short, terminal catkin; with deciduous bracts, a small membrane enclosing each flower; nut, oblong, included in a large, bladder-like membrane.

Ostrya Virginica—Iron Wood.

The Iron Wood belongs to the northern parts of the United States and the British Provinces. It sometimes, though rarely, grows to the height of forty feet. The wood is heavy, compact and fine-grained. It is used for beetles, mallets, cogs of mill wheels, etc. Its slow growth and inferior size render it ineligible for culture as a timber tree. As an ornamental tree it is pretty, with light, graceful spray. It is propagated by seed sown in spring.

OXYDENDRUM.

Natural Order, Ericaceæ.

Calyx without bractlets, of five almost distinct sepals; valvate in the bud; corolla, ovate, five-toothed; stamens, ten; anthers, fixed near the base, linear, awnless, the cells tapering upwards and opening by a long chink; pod, oblong, pyramidal, five-celled, five-valved; seeds, all ascending, slender.

Oxydendrum arboreum—Sorrel Tree.

This tree is found from Ohio and Pennsylvania, southward, principally along the Alleghany mountains. It grows to the height of from forty to sixty feet. It begins to produce flowers when only five or six feet high. They are in terminal panicles, and appear in August. The wood is of little value, but for ornamental purposes, this tree well deserves notice. It is hardy much farther north than its native localities.

PAULOWNIA.

Natural Order—Scrophulariaceæ.

Calyx, five-cleft; segments, equal, coriaceous, covered with a rusty down; corolla, two-lipped, imbricated in its æstivation, the two upper lobes external; fruit, ovate, with a sharp point.

Paulownia imperialis is the only known species. It is a native of Japan, and was introduced not more than twenty-five or thirty years since. It is a very rapid grower, with large, rough leaves, and large clusters of sky-blue flowers. These appear in June, and by their beauty compensate for the coarseness of their foliage. It is hardy about the city of New York, but farther north it is said that the blossom buds, which are quite conspicuous after the leaves have fallen, are often killed during the winter. In the rich soils of Northern Illinois it makes a rank, succulent growth, which is invariably killed to the ground the following winter. It will grow seven or eight feet the second year, from the seed, with leaves two feet broad. Where the climate is not too severe, it is a desirable tree. It is easily propagated by cuttings of the roots, or by seed sown in spring. The seed is produced in a cone-shaped capsule, and is furnished with a membraneous wing.

PLATANUS—PLANE TREE.

Natural Order, Platanaceæ.

Sterile flowers, of numerous stamens, with little scales intermixed; fertile flowers in separate catkins, consisting of inversely pyramidal ovaries, mixed with little scales; style, lateral, simple; nutlets, coriaceous, small, tawny, hairy below, containing a single seed.

Platanus occidentalis—Plane, Sycamore, Buttonwood.

Leaves, angularly sinuate, lobed or toothed, the short lobes sharp-pointed; fertile heads, solitary, on a long peduncle.

The Plane Tree is common throughout the northern, middle, and western States. It is found on the banks of rivers, and attains a greater size than any other deciduous tree in North America. Its wood is not valuable. It is little esteemed for fuel, is difficult to split, is very liable to warp, and speedily decays if exposed to the weather. It is sometimes sawed into square timber and planks, to be used where they can be kept dry. As a timber tree, it is not worth cultivation. It was formerly valued as a shade tree, but is now less esteemed on account of a disease, apparently a sort of blight, which often greatly disfigures it. The seeds, with the plumy tufts by which they are surmounted, are compacted together in the form of a ball, about an inch in diameter. They may be sown when ripe, or kept till spring. In the latter case, it is best to soak them before sowing. The tree may be propagated by cuttings of the last year's wood.

The Tulip Tree.

P. Orientalis, the Asiatic Plane, much resembles the American species, but is not very common in this country. It is said to be free from disease.

POPULUS—POPLAR, ASPEN.

Natural Order, Salicaceæ.

Bracts of the catkins irregularly cut, lobed at the apex; flowers, from a cup-shaped disk, which is obliquely lengthened in front; stamens, eight to thirty, or more; filaments, distinct; stigmas, elongated; buds covered with a resinous varnish; aments long and drooping, appearing before the leaves.

There are many species of the Poplar, most of them growing to a large size. A strong family likeness exists among them in general appearance, foliage, and quality of their wood. In Europe, the wood of some kinds of Poplar is used for a variety of purposes, and is considerably esteemed, but in America, where many better kinds of timber are found, it is considered of less value. Most species of the Poplar grow rapidly, a quality which appears to be their principal recommendation; but in this respect they are equalled by more valuable trees. As fuel, their wood ranks among the poorest, although, when properly dried, it answers very well for kindling wood and for summer use. Some species are planted for shade, but for this purpose the female tree should be always avoided, as the cottony-down with which the seeds are winged becomes a great annoyance. The Poplars grow readily from cuttings, and are seldom propagated in

11

any other way. Stakes set in the ground close enough to form a fence will take root, and last till the trees become so crowded that a part will die.

1. *Populus monilifera—Cottonwood.*

Young branches slightly angled, becoming round; leaves broadly deltoid, with spreading, prominent nerves, slightly heart-shaped or truncate at the base, taper-pointed, serrate; fertile catkins very long; scales fringed, not hairy.

The Cottonwood grows in the Atlantic States, but is most common in the Mississippi valley, in which it is everywhere found along the banks of streams. It is often an annoyance to farmers, by springing up in cultivated grounds that are somewhat moist. It becomes a large tree, eighty feet high, or more. The wood is white and soft, and the fibres are usually so interwoven that it is very difficult to split it. It is sometimes sawed into planks and boards, but such is its disposition to warp that it is difficult to keep them in place when used. It is sometimes planted for shade, but is liable to the objection that it often casts its leaves before frosts occur. When planted near buildings, only the male tree should be used; the female sheds its down in such quantities as to become a nuisance.

2. *Populus angulata—Angled Cottonwood.*

Branches, acutely angled or winged; leaves, broadly deltoid or heart-ovate, smooth, crenate, serrate, or with obtuse, cartilaginous teeth.

This is also a large and lofty tree, and grows in the same soils and situations as the preceding, which it greatly resembles. So much are they alike, that they are not only confounded by the Western people generally, but some botanists are strongly inclined to doubt the existence of more than one species.

There is a variety called the Yellow Cottonwood, which is not uncommon, the heart-wood of which is of a yellowish color, like that of the Tulip Tree. It grows in the same situations as others of its kind, and is split without difficulty into rails. Shingles have been manufactured from it, which lasted a considerable time. When sawed into lumber, it does not warp, like the Cottonwood generally. If P. angulata and P. monilifera are really distinct, it is a matter of uncertainty to which this variety belongs. The subject deserves investigation.

3. *P. tremuloides—American Aspen.*

Leaves, roundish, heart-shaped, with a short, sharp point, and small, regular teeth, smooth on both sides, with downy margins; scales cut into three or four deep linear divisions, fringed with long hairs.

This species of Poplar is abundant in the British Provinces, and common in the northern part of the United States. It seldom exceeds thirty feet in height, and is a short-lived tree. The wood resembles that of other species.

4. *Populus grandidentata—Large Aspen.*

Leaves, roundish-ovate, sinuately toothed with large, unequal teeth, very downy when young, afterwards smooth on both sides.

This tree grows in the same localities as the preceding, but is of larger size and more rapid growth. It is easily distinguished by its larger leaves, which are coarsely toothed, and covered with a white, silky down when they first appear. The tree is sometimes hewn into square timber, which is used where it can be kept dry. It has considerable strength, and does not readily spring or settle. When large enough, it is sawed into lumber, which is employed in the finishing of houses, and does not warp easily. This, and the preceding species, are used in Northern Illinois for making fences—the trees being cut into lengths of eight feet, split when of proper size, and nailed upon posts. If cut in June or July, and peeled, these rails will last twelve or fifteen years, but if the bark be not removed, they very speedily decay.

5. *Populus neterophylla—Downy-leaved Poplar.*

Branches, round; leaves, heart-shaped, or roundish-ovate, obtuse, serrate, white, woolly when young, at length nearly smooth, except on the veins beneath.

This species appears to be rare in the Northern States. It is found in Southern Illinois, but my acquaintance with it is slight. It is a tree of considerable size, and does not seem to be at all valued for its timber where it grows.

6. *Populus balsamifera—Balsam Poplar, Tacmahac.*

Branches, round, leaves ovate, gradually tapering and pointed, finely serrate, smooth on both sides, whitish beneath; scales dilated, slightly hairy.

This Poplar, which is a large and lofty tree, is said to be rare within the limits of the United States, but is common in the countries north. I have never met with it. The timber is said to be little used where it is most abundant. A variety of this species, P. candicans (Balm of Gilead), which is a small tree, is common in cultivation, and its buds are used for medicinal purposes.

7. *Populus alba—White Poplar, Abele.*

Leaves, lobed and toothed, somewhat heart-shaped at the base, snow-white, and densely downy beneath; stigmas, four.

The White or Silver-leaved Poplar has been widely disseminated in the United States as an ornamental tree. Planted on lawns, it becomes a nuisance, from the number of suckers which it throws up from its roots. It is, however, desirable as a street tree in towns and cities, where its disposition to sucker is not objectionable, since, like other Poplars, it endures smoke and dust better than most trees.

Michaux describes the White Poplar as one of the largest trees of the Eastern continent, growing to the height of ninety or one hundred feet, with a diameter of five or six feet. Of the wood he says: "It is superior to that of other species of Poplar in whiteness, in fineness and in strength; it gives a firmer hold to nails, and is not liable to split or warp. In England and Belgium it is commonly used by turners for bowls, trays, etc. In the South of France it is employed for the floors and wainscots of houses; and in Paris, for the cases in which goods are packed for exportation."

Michaux recommends this species as the best substitute for the Tulip Tree, and advises its cultivation in the United States. It is undoubtedly superior to any of our native Poplars, and merits the attention of planters, more particularly on the plains towards the Rocky mountains. It is propagated with greater ease and rapidity than the Tulip Tree; it grows more rapidly, and will endure a colder climate. It may be propagated by slips, suckers, or by branches five or six feet long and two or three inches in diameter. When the latter are used, the larger end should be sharpened by a sloping cut on one side to expose the bark, and set fifteen or eighteen inches in the ground. The disposition of the tree to sucker would be no objection in forest culture.

Populus dilatata, the Lombardy Poplar, is well known, and has been introduced everywhere as an ornamental tree. In this country it is of little value for any other purpose, and not worth much even for that.

PRUNUS—PLUM CHERRY.

Natural Order, Rosaceæ.

Calyx, five-cleft; petals, five, spreading; stamens, fifteen to thirty; ovary with two pendulous ovules; berry, fleshy; the stone smooth and even.

1. *Prunus serotina — Wild Black Cherry.*

Leaves, oblong or lanceolate-oblong, taper-pointed, serrate, with in-curved, short and callous teeth, thickish, shining above; racemes, elongated; petals, obovate; fruit, purplish-black.

The Wild Cherry is found throughout the northern half of the United States east of the Rocky mountains, and, in favorable situations, becomes a very large tree. Although the soil and climate are well suited to its growth, it is rarely found of very considerable size in the neighborhood of the prairies of Illinois and Iowa. The reason appears to be, that the fires which formerly ravaged these regions destroyed it more easily than the Oaks and Hickories. It is found in the Southern States along the Alleghany mountains. The wood is highly esteemed for cabinet work, and was formerly preferred to the Black Walnut. I have seen old houses in which Wild Cherry had been principally employed for the interior woodwork. But the large stocks which once abounded in the forests of many parts of the country are now very rarely seen, except in remote and thinly settled districts. The wood is of a light red color, becoming darker with age; it is compact, fine-grained and not liable to warp.

The Wild Cherry is a fine ornamental tree, but is liable to the objection, that, in open grounds, it is more likely to be infested by the tent caterpillar than even the Apple Tree. When growing in groves or forests, I have seldom if ever seen it attacked by this insect. Like some other kinds of timber, it is not particularly valuable until it has attained a considerable size; nevertheless, it merits the attention of those who may plant for posterity. It should be thickly grown, and the thinnings will make good fuel. The fruit is produced abundantly while the trees are yet small. It ripens in August. When gathered for sowing, the seed must not be allowed to become dry, but should be mixed with sand and sown either in the fall or spring.

2. *Prunus Pennsylvanica—Wild Red Cherry.*

Leaves, oblong-lanceolate, pointed finely and sharply serrate, shining, green and smooth both sides; flowers, many in a cluster, on long pedicels; fruit, round, light red.

This species is common only in the most northern States of the Union, and in the Provinces of the Dominion. Its ordinary height does not exceed twenty or thirty feet. I have sometimes seen trees forty feet high and one foot in diameter, but such are very rare. The wood is of a light red color, and not inferior to that of the preceding species for cabinet work; but is seldom used for that purpose, on account of its inferior size.

In the countries where it is common, the Red Cherry springs up spontaneously wherever the land has been cleared or the forest ravaged by fire. The cultivated kinds of Cherry grow readily when budded or grafted on it. It is the only native species upon which they will succeed.

PYRUS.

Natural Order, Rosaceæ.

Calyx, tube urn-shaped, five-cleft; petals, roundish or obovate; stamens, numerous; styles, two to five; fruit, fleshy or berry-like.

Pyrus aucuparia—European Mountain Ash.

Leaves, pinnate, glabrous; leaflets, serrate; flowers, corymbose; fruit, round, small, red.

The European Mountain Ash grows to the height of thirty feet, and sometimes considerably exceeds that stature. It is much cultivated for ornament, for which its fine foliage, clusters of white flowers and red berries eminently qualify it. It rarely needs pruning, and never grows out of shape. It may be used as a stock on which to graft the Pear. It is liable to be attacked by the apple borer (saperda bivittata), and where that insect is common, requires the same care to guard against it as the Apple Tree.

For propagation, the berries, when ripe, may be put in a cask or box and kept moist until they are sufficiently decayed to allow the seed to be washed out easily. The seed is then mixed with sand and put in a place where it will freeze until spring. Unless the berries undergo a fermentation, the seed is not likely to grow the first year. Loudon says the mode practiced in Britain is to mix the berries with fine sand, and lay them in beds a foot thick, covering them with two or three inches of sand, and allowing them to remain for one year. They are then taken up, the sand sifted out, and the berries sown. If kept till spring, the seed must be sown early, as, when ready to germinate, it will do so at a lower temperature than most other seeds. When the young plants appear they should be shaded from the hot sunshine.

P. Americana, the American Mountain Ash, greatly resembles the European, and is by some considered a variety, but never becomes so large a tree. It is propagated in the same manner. The two may be distinguished while small by the buds, which in the European are downy, but in the American viscous or sticky.

Pyrus coronaria—American Crab-apple.

Leaves, ovate, often rather heart-shaped, cut-serrate or lobed, soon glabrous; styles, woolly and united at the base.

The Crabapple is found in many parts of the United States, and is very common on the borders of the western prairies. Its ordinary height is fifteen or twenty feet, but it is sometimes larger. It is a handsome ornamental tree, with rose-colored fragrant flowers. The wood is similar to that of the common Apple; the fruit is of no value. The tree should be transplanted while small.' It is easily propagated from seed, like the common Apple Tree.

QUERCUS—OAK.

Natural Order, Cupuliferæ.

Sterile flowers clustered in catkins, without bracts; calyx, six to eight-parted; stamens, six to twelve;

anthers, two-celled; fertile flowers consisting of a three-celled and six-ovuled ovary, with a three-lobed stigma, enclosed by a scaly involucre, becoming a cup around the base of the acorn; flowers, greenish or yellowish, the fertile ones inconspicuous.

With, perhaps, the exception of the Coniferous tribe, there is no tree so generally useful to mankind as the Oak. The species are quite numerous. Loudon describes more than forty that have been cultivated in Great Britain, and gives some account of seventy or eighty more. Others have been since discovered. With few exceptions, they are of considerable size, and belong mostly to temperate climates, those growing within the tropics being found in elevated situations. The multiplication and distribution of the Oak appear to be in proportion to its usefulness, since most countries of Europe and North America are known to possess one or more species affording timber of superior excellence. Many of them are trees of majestic appearance and great beauty, and merit greater attention for ornamental purposes than they have yet received.

In the present work, a part only of the native Oaks of the United States will be noticed, selecting principally such as are well-known and most valuable. Most species are of rather slow growth, and if land owners could be induced to interest themselves in the subject, more might be accomplished in many parts of the country by the preservation of young trees already in existence, than could be expected to result in a considerable time from artificial plantations. In the prairie regions of the West, young wood, principally Oak, springs up on the bluffs and broken lands along the streams when fires are excluded, and only needs protection ultimately to become valuable timber.

In many of the oaks, the form of the leaves varies so much with different conditions of the tree or different stages of its growth, that it constitutes an uncertain characteristic by which to distinguish the species. Consequently, where the wood is similar, different species are sometimes confounded under one name. The fructification affords a more certain mode of distinction.

The Oaks are propagated almost exclusively by seed, grafting and layering being employed only for the increase of particular varieties. The acorns fall in October, and should be collected before they become dry, mixed with sufficient sand to prevent heating, and kept damp in a cool place until sown. This may be done in autumn or in early spring. The latter is safest, as they are sometimes taken out by mice and squirrels in the winter. It seems to be the prevalent opinion that it is best to plant the acorns where the trees are to remain, though there are not wanting those among the tree planters of Europe who maintain that it is best to transplant them. The best mode of treatment appears to be to plant tho acorns one foot apart in alternate rows, planting corn, potatoes, or beans in the intermediate rows. This should be continued for at least three years, after which the vacant rows should be planted with Silver

Maple, Willow, or some other tree easily raised. In England, trees planted in this way among Oaks are termed nurses, though there the practice is to plant the nurses first. The Scotch Pine is preferred as a nurse by many, as the protection it affords is thought to accelerate the growth of the Oaks.

1. *Quercus alba — White Oak.*

Mature leaves, smooth, pale or glabrous underneath, bright green above, obovate-oblong, cut into three to nine lobes; cup, hemispherical, saucer-shaped, rough or tubercled at maturity, naked, much shorter than the acorn.

The White Oak is found in most parts of the United States east of the Mississippi, although in some sections it is by no means abundant. It is said to be rare in Kansas and Nebraska, where the Chincapin, or Yellow Oak (Q. castanea), takes its place. In the States of Illinois and Iowa, it is seldom found upon the richest soils. It most commonly grows upon a yellow or ash-colored loam of moderate fertility. A belt of this kind of soil, with a surface more or less uneven, extends along the streams between the bottom lands and the prairies, and also occurs in other localities. On this soil the White Oak constitutes the principal growth of timber.

When fully developed, the White Oak is one of the largest and noblest trees of its genus, and with, perhaps, the exception of the White Pine, is the most useful tree found in the United States. Wherever strength, compactness, and durability are required, its wood is preferred to that of any other tree, except the Live Oak of the Southern States. It is more abundant than any other species of oak in Northern and Central Illinois, but the forests are in the course of rapid destruction, and the attention of land owners cannot be too soon directed to the preservation of such as remain, and the formation of new plantations.

Although the White Oak is not often met with upon the richest soils of the Western States, it will, nevertheless, flourish on them. It is accounted a slow grower, but does not, like some other trees, slacken its growth as it becomes larger. The multiplied uses to which it is applied are too well-known to need enumeration, and its extensive culture cannot be too strongly recommended.

2. *Quercus macrocarpa—Bur Oak, Overcup Oak.*

Leaves, lyrate-obovate, or oblong, downy beneath, deeply and sinuately lobed, the lobes obtuse and spreading; cup, deep, scaly and fringed; acorns, large, ovate.

This species is much more abundant west of the Alleghanies than in the Atlantic States. It is a large and handsome tree, with larger leaves than any other American species. It is commonly found on richer soils than the White Oak, which it equals in size, and for most purposes in the excellence of its wood. Michaux speaks disparagingly of the quality of its timber, but it appears quite probable that he had but little acquaintance with it. It certainly is equally as strong, tough and elastic as the White Oak. It is considered not less valuable in the manufacture of agricultural implements and machinery, and is more durable, as has been proved in its use for posts. In one respect it is inferior; its pores are so open as to render it unfit for casks designed to contain oils or spirits. It is a fine tree for landscape ornament, and its cultivation as a timber tree is unhesitatingly recommended.

3. *Quercus obtusiloba—Post Oak.*

Leaves, grayish, downy underneath, pale and rough above, thickish, sinuately lobed, the upper lobes the largest; cup, saucer-shaped, naked, one-third the length of the ovoid acorn.

In the Atlantic States, the Post Oak grows mostly upon poor, dry soils, and is said to be most abundant in Maryland and Virginia. It is common in Central and Southern Illinois, on what are, or rather were, called Post Oak barrens. These are tracts of land with an undulating surface, a soil of yellow, clayey loam, and, at the first settlement of the country, covered with a scattered growth of Post Oak, intermingled with White Oak and the Shellbark and Mockernut Hickory. It is seldom more than forty or fifty feet high, with a diameter of twelve to eighteen inches. It is much inclined to branch, even when closely grown, and rarely furnishes timber of considerable length. The acorns are small, and very sweet. The wood is yellowish, strong and fine-grained, and more durable than the White Oak. It is consequently preferred for posts, wagon wheels, and wherever durable timber is desired. The valuable properties of its wood indicate this species as one of those deserving propagation in the forests of the United States.

4. *Quercus prinus—Swamp Chestnut Oak.*

Leaves, obovate, or oblong-obovate, coarsely-toothed, downy beneath, smooth above; cup, hemispherical, thick-tubercled, one-third the length of the acorn.

This species of Oak is found growing in low grounds, from Pennsylvania southward. It is a large, lofty and beautiful tree. It grows to the height of eighty or ninety feet, with a trunk of uniform diameter for fifty feet. Its timber is inferior to that of the preceding three species, but better than most of those of biennial fructification. It grows almost exclusively in rich bottom lands.

Variety *Q. p. monticola* (Rock Chestnut Oak), grows in rocky or hilly woodlands, mostly along the Alleghanies. The wood is so heavy as to sink in water, and is of superior quality to the species.

Variety *Q. p. discolor* (Swamp White Oak), leaves unequally and more deeply sinuate-toothed, often almost sinuate-pinnatifid, whitish downy beneath, bright green above; cup with the scales more pointed, the upper sometimes awned, and forming a fringed margin; acorns, one inch or less long. This is a marked variety, found farther north than the Chestnut Oak, and affords wood of a better quality. It is found in low grounds throughout the State of

Illinois, and in most other parts of the Northern States. The wood is esteemed next to that of the White Oak.

5. *Quercus castanea—Chincapin Oak, Yellow Chestnut Oak.*

Leaves, oblong-lanceolate or oblong-acute, white and slightly downy beneath, sharply-toothed; cup thin, acorn small.

In the Western States this tree is called the Chincapin Oak—a name which is likewise applied to a dwarf species, common in the Atlantic States. It is a tall, handsome tree, reaching the height of sixty or seventy feet, but usually rather slender. It grows in rich, cool soils, and is oftener found in valleys than elsewhere. The bark resembles that of the White Oak; the leaves are much like those of the Chestnut; the acorns are quite small and very sweet. The wood is of a yellowish color, hard, strong and durable. It is said to be more common in Kansas and Nebraska than in Illinois. It is undoubtedly worthy of cultivation, but it is so thinly disseminated in most countries where it is native, that it would not be easy to procure any considerable quantity of seed.

All the above described species ripen their fruit the first year.

6. *Quercus tinctoria—Black Oak.*

Leaves, more or less rusty, pubescent when young, nearly smooth when old, obovate-oblong, deeply sinuate; cup turbinate; acorn nearly round, or depressed-globular.

The Black Oak is found in most parts of the United States, both east and west of the Alleghanies. It flourishes in poorer soils than the White Oak, but is not unfrequently found growing in company with it. It is one of the largest and loftiest of the Oak family, being sometimes eighty or ninety feet in height, and four or five feet in diameter. It is the only kind of Oak growing on the barren sand ridges in the neighborhood of marshes in some parts of Illinois.

The wood is coarse grained, but possesses considerable strength and durability, and is more esteemed than any of the species hereafter mentioned, except the Live Oak. The inner bark, called quercitron, is much used for dyeing. The bark is also used for tanning, and the wood is excellent fuel.

This, and the species hereafter described, ripen their fruit biennially. With one or two exceptions, the quality of their timber is inferior to that of those species which perfect their fruit in one year.

7. *Quercus coccinea—Scarlet Oak.*

Leaves on long petioles, oblong, deeply sinuate-lobed, with broad and open sinuses, smooth and shiny both sides, the lobes divergent, toothed; acorn, ovid or globular, one-half to three-fourths of an inch long.

This is a large and lofty tree, the foliage and fruit of which considerably resemble those of the Black

Oak; in fact, some botanists are disposed to consider the latter as merely a variety of this species. The leaves turn to a bright red in the fall—the acorns have a white kernel, not yellowish, as in the Black Oak. The wood is of inferior quality, both for fuel and other purposes. In some parts of the country, this species is confunded with the Red Oak, in others with the Spanish Oak. It cannot be recommended for propagation.

8. *Quercus rubra—Red Oak.*

Leaves, oblong, smooth, pale beneath, sinutely cut with rather narrow sinuses into short, spreading lobes, four to six on a side; acorn large, ovoid or oblong.

The Red Oak is well-known in most parts of the United States, and is one of the most common species in Illinois. It will grow on poor soils, but is most at home on those that are fertile. It grows more rapidly than most other kinds of Oak, and sometimes reaches the height of eighty feet, with a proportionate diameter.

The wood is coarse-grained, of reddish color, with open pores, and not very durable. It is much inferior to the Black Oak, and is little esteemed, although considerably used where better timber is not abundant. It is a very handsome ornamental tree.

9. *Quercus palustris—Pin Oak.*

Leaves, oblong, smooth and shining, bright green both sides, deeply pinnatifid, with broad and rounded sinuses, the lobes divergent, cut-lobed, and toothed, acute; acorn, small, round.

The Pin Oak is a handsome tree, with a conical head, and light, elegant foliage. It often becomes a tree of very considerable size, and is commonly found in moist grounds. It will, nevertheless, thrive in dry soils. The wood is coarse grained, with large, open pores; it is stronger and tougher than that of the Red and Scarlet Oaks, but not very durable. It is sometimes planted for ornament.

10. *Quercus Phellos — Willow Oak.*

Leaves, linear, lanceolate, narrowed to both ends, smooth, light green; acorn, small; kernel, orange color.

This species appears to be confined to the maritime parts of the Atlantic States; it is rarely if ever found far in the interior. It grows to the height of fifty or sixty feet, and is remarkable for the form of its leaves, which resemble those of the Willow. The wood is strong, but coarse grained, and of little durability. As fuel, it ranks among the poorest. It is not abundant in its native localities. The singularity of its foliage may recommend it to the amateur, but it does not merit cultivation for any useful purpose.

11. *Quercus imbricaria—Laurel Oak.*

Leaves, lanceolate-oblong, acute, smooth and shining above, somewhat downy beneath; acorn, globular.

This species of oak grows principally in open situations, and is very common on the skirts of the Illinois prairies. It is seldom found in the midst of dense forests. It is a middle-sized tree, reaching the height of fifty or sixty feet, with a diameter of two feet. Its foliage is handsome, resembling that of the Mountain Laurel, whence its name. The wood is coarse-grained, and not valuable. It is split into rails —is sometimes used in the frames of houses, and was formerly manufactured into shingles, for which it is an indifferent material.

12. *Quercus nigra—Black Jack Oak.*

Leaves, broadly wedge-shaped, rounded at the base, slightly three to five-lobed at the end, rusty beneath, shining above, large; cup, top-shaped, covering half the acorn.

The Black Jack Oak is commonly found in poor soils. It is a small tree, seldom exceeding thirty feet in height. The trunk is generally crooked. The wood is more esteemed for fuel than that of any other species of oak; and this is almost the only use to which it is applied.

13. *Quercus falcata—Spanish Oak.*

Leaves, grayish, downy beneath, obtuse, or rounded at the base, three to five-lobed above; the lobes prolonged, mostly narrow, and more or less scythe-shaped, especially the terminal one; cup, saucer-shaped; acorn, spherical.

The Spanish Oak appears to be somewhat rare in the Mississippi valley. It is found in Southern Illinois. It is common in the maritime parts of the Middle and Southern States, and in favorable situations becomes a large tree. Its foliage is very variable. The wood much resembles that of the Red Oak, to which it is in no respect superior.

14. *Quercus virens—Live Oak.*

Leaves, obtuse, coriaceous, oblong or elliptical, hoary beneath; cup, top-shaped; acorn, oblong.

The Live Oak belongs to the Southern States, and grows only near the sea coast. It is found within the limits of this work on the coast of Virginia. Further south it becomes a large tree. The wood is invaluable, being more esteemed for ship-building than that of any other tree.

Quercus suber, the Cork Oak, was recommended by Michaux for cultivation in the Southern States. It would probably succeed in North Carolina and Tennessee. Like the Live Oak, it is evergreen.

There are three or four species of dwarf Oaks found in the United States, but they are of little value for any purpose whatever.

ROBINIA—LOCUST.

Natural Order, Leguminosæ.

Calyx, short, five-toothed, slightly two-lipped; standard, large, rounded, turned back; pod, linear, flat, several-seeded, margined on the seed-bearing edge · two-valved.

1. *Robinia Pseudacacia—Common Locust.*

Branches, naked; racemes, slender, loose; flowers, white, fragrant; pod, smooth.

The Locust is commonly a middle-sized tree, but, according to Michaux, it grows in Kentucky and West Tennessee to the height of seventy or eighty feet, with a diameter of four feet. It has been widely disseminated for ornament, and occasionally planted for the sake of its very valuable timber. As an ornamental tree, it is very handsome while young, but becomes ugly as it increases in age. The wood is hard, compact, and strong, and resists decay longer than almost any other kind of timber. It is employed in ship-building whenever it can be obtained, and is highly valued for that purpose. It is also used for posts, which are more lasting than any others, excepting those of the Red Mulberry. In a stick of Locust timber, the proportion of sap-wood is very small.

There are varieties of the Locust, named White, Yellow, and Black Locust, differing principally in the durability of the wood. Some have supposed this difference to be caused by the different soils in which they grow, but this does not appear to be the case. The Yellow Locust grown on Long Island was introduced from North Carolina about one hundred years since, and is most esteemed. This variety produces seed very sparingly. The White Locust, so called from the color of the heart, grows in similar soils, and is not very durable. It is sometimes called Seed Locust, from the abundance of seed which it produces. The Black Locust grows in the Western States, and is esteemed for its durability.

Between 1855 and 1865, a species of borer (Arhopalus robiniæ) peculiar to the Locust, spread over the State of Illinois, destroying nearly every tree of the kind in the country. Not only were trees planted for shade attacked, but groves grown for timber were completely ruined. With the disappearance of the trees the insect disappeared also, and for several years the few trees which survived, as well as those which have since sprung up from seed, or from the roots of the old trees, have been untouched by it.

The rapid growth of the Locust, and the invaluable qualities of its wood, recommend it strongly to the attention of cultivators. For ornamental purposes, there are many trees better deserving culture; the suckers it throws up from its roots, and its thin, scraggy appearance when it has attained a considerable size, constitute strong objections to it.

The Locust may be propagated by suckers, but is best grown from seed sown in the spring. It is usually prepared for sowing by pouring boiling water upon it, and allowing it to stand till cool. It should then be sown immediately.

2. *Robinia viscosa—Clammy Locust.*

Branchlets and leaf-stalks clammy; flowers crowded with oblong racemes, tinged with rose color.

This is a smaller tree than the preceding, growing to the height of thirty or forty feet. The properties of its wood are nearly the same as in the preceding species, but its inferior size renders it less desirable for forest culture. Its foliage is thick, its flowers are numerous, of a beautiful rose-color, and are sometimes produced twice in the season. They are not fragrant. Like the Common Locust, it is of rapid growth, produces numerous suckers from its roots, and is liable to the attacks of the same insect. It is propagated like the preceding.

Robinia hispida, the Rose Acacia, is a shrub commonly cultivated for the beauty of its flowers. It is said to be increased in size by grafting on the other species.

SALIX—WILLOW.

Natural Order, Salicaceæ.

Catkins, with the scales entire; sterile flowers of three to six stamens, with one or two small glands; pistillate flowers, with a small, flat gland at the base of the ovary on the inner side.

There are many species of the Willow, and a considerable number are natives of the United States; but most of these are mere shrubs, and not one of them is applied to any useful purpose. A few foreign species have been introduced, possessing qualities which render them worthy of cultivation. All the Willows grow readily from cuttings, and are seldom propagated in any other way.

1. *Salix alba—White Willow.*

Leaves, lanceolate, pointed, toothed, covered with white, silky hairs, especially beneath; stipules, lanceolate; stigmas, nearly sessile, thick and recurved.

The White Willow is a handsome tree, which in moist situations grows to the height of seventy or eighty feet, with a proportionate diameter. It will thrive in dry soils, but does not become so large. It is a very rapid grower, and its culture has been strongly recommended for screens to break the force of the wind on the prairies of the West. Several years since, some itinerant speculators succeeded in "raising the wind," and producing quite an excitement in regard to its merits as a hedge plant. Stories of its excellence for this and other purposes were circulated, so extravagant as to show that their authors counted largely upon the gullibility of the community. Great quantities of cuttings were sold at high prices in Illinois and Iowa, and unless some of the sharpers were much belied, native Willows were cut from the swamps, and sold as the White Willow. As a matter of course, a reaction soon took place, and the White Willow is now wholly neglected. An impenetrable fence may undoubtedly be soon formed by planting it closely, but its permanence is quite another matter. When trees of so large size are crowded thickly together, a part necessarily soon perish.

The wood of the White Willow is light and soft, and speedily decays when exposed to alternations of dryness and moisture, or when placed in contact with the earth. When grown thickly in plantations, it produces long straight poles, which, cut to the proper length, and nailed upon posts, make a good fence, and will last a considerable time. It is not needful, as in the case of the poplar, to remove the bark. The wood may be applied to other uses, and the tree is unquestionably desirable for planting on farms in the open prairies, wherever it is an object to produce trees for shelter, and wood for use in the shortest possible time. In Maryland and Delaware it is grown for making charcoal, which is employed in the manufacture of gunpowder. In Europe the bark is used for tanning.

Salix vitellina, the Golden Willow, is a variety of this species, and differs principally in the color of the bark, and somewhat more spreading growth.

2. *Salix fragilis—Brittle Willow.*

Leaves, lanceolate, taper-pointed, smooth, glaucous beneath, slightly silky when young, serrate, with inflexed teeth; stipules, half-heart shaped; stamens, commonly two.

This species, which is said to grow to the height of ninety feet, is less widely distributed in the United States than the White Willow. It is cultivated for basket work. A variety, Russelliana (Bedford Willow), is considered in Great Britain the most valuable of the Willows for timber.

3. *Salix Babylonica—Weeping Willow.*

Leaves, lanceolate, acuminate, serrate, smooth, glaucous beneath.

The Weeping Willow is a well known tree, cultivated only for ornament. On the shores of lakes and ponds, or beside streams, it is very appropriate, if not too profusely planted. Very large trees of this species are met with on Long Island. In Northern Illinois it is frequently killed to the ground by the severity of the winters.

The American Weeping Willow, a variety of the Salix purpurea, and the Kilmarnock Weeping Willow, a variety of Salix caprea, are grafted several feet from the ground on other species, as they will not rise to a tree if grown from cuttings. They are quite hardy.

4. *Salix lucida—Shining Willow.*

Leaves, ovate-oblong, or lanceolate, and narrow, with a long, tapering point, smooth and shining on both sides, serrate; stipules, oblong, toothed; stamens, five.

This is a native species, and the most ornamental of the genus. It grows to the height of fifteen or twenty feet in cultivation, but in its native localities is commonly of smaller size. It is frequent along the mountain streams of New England, and is easily recognized by its leaves, which shine as though coated with varnish. I have never seen it in the Western States.

Salix viminalis, and two or three other foreign species of Osier Willow, are cultivated for basket work.

SASSAFRAS.

Natural Order, Lauraceæ.

Flowers, diœcious, with a six-parted calyx; the sterile with nine stamens inserted on the base of the calyx, in three rows, the three inner with a pair of stalked glands at the base of each; anthers, four-celled, four-valved; fertile flowers with six rudiments of stamens and an ovoid ovary; berry, ovoid, blue.

Sassafras officinale—Sassafras.

Leaves, ovate, entire, or some of them three-lobed, soon smooth; buds and pedicels, downy.

The Sassafras is common over a large portion of the United States. It varies greatly in size in different situations. Growing in poor soils, or produced by suckers from the roots of old trees, it seldom attains a considerable magnitude. It reaches its full development only in rich soils. I have seen it in the State of Mississippi, three feet in diameter; and it was formerly sometimes found of large size in the forests of Illinois. The wood is not very strong, but is fine-grained and durable. It is valuable for cabinet work, but is not much used for that purpose on account of the scarcity of stocks sufficiently large. It is said that bedsteads made of it are never infested by vermin.

The bark of the root was formerly highly valued, and much used for medicinal purposes, but is at present less esteemed. It is a handsome ornamental tree, and will thrive in any good soil that is not wet. It is propagated by suckers, or by seeds, which should be put in the ground when ripe. They will not, however, always vegetate the first year.

SHEPHERDIA.

Natural Order, Elæagnaceæ.

Flowers, diœcious, the sterile with a four-parted calyx, and eight stamens; the fertile with an urn-shaped, four-cleft calyx, enclosing the ovary, and becoming berry-like in fruit.

Shepherdia argentea—Buffalo Berry.

Leaves, oblong-ovate, smooth on both sides, and covered with silvery pellate scales.

The Buffalo Berry is a native of the country on the Upper Missouri, and west of the Rocky Mountains. In cultivation, it becomes a tree twenty-five or thirty feet high. It is cultivated principally for its fruit, which is produced in abundance, and if not gathered, will remain on the branches through the winter. It resembles small, red currants, but is of richer taste, and literally covers the twigs and branches. It is esteemed for pies, tarts and preserves. The tree is strictly diœcious, and in order to obtain fruit, both sexes must be grown not far from each other. It is quite hardy in the northern part of the United States. In growth it resembles the Buckthorn, and would probably make as good a hedge. It is propagated by suckers or by seed, which should be washed from the berries and laid by until spring.

SOPHORA.

Natural Order, Leguminosæ.

Calyx, five-toothed; legume, necklace-shaped, many-seeded; leaf with more than three leaflets.

Sophora Japonica—Japan Sophora.

Leaves, pinnate; leaflets, many, ovate, smooth; panicle, terminal; pods, smooth.

The Sophora is a native of Japan and China. It is a middle-sized tree, sometimes growing to the height of sixty feet. It somewhat resembles the locust, but is a handsomer tree; and its flowers, which it produces in August, although smaller, are more abundant. Little is known respecting the quality of the wood, as the tree is not very common, and grown only for ornament. It is, however, said to equal that of the Locust in durability, and to be as hard and compact as that of the Box. The tree makes slow progress in the rich loam of the Illinois prairies, its growth being checked by mildew on the young shoots. In favorable situations it is said to grow rapidly. It is commonly propagated by layers, but is best grown from seed when it can be procured.

TILIA.

Natural Order, Tiliaceæ.

Sepals, five; petals, five, spatulate-oblong; stamens, numerous; pistil with a five-celled ovary, with two ovules in each; style, one; stigma, five-toothed; nut, coriaceous, one-celled, one or two-seeded.

1. *Tilia Americana—Lynn, Linden, Basswood.*

Leaves, green and smooth, or nearly so, somewhat thick.

This tree is found in all the Northern and Middle States, and southward along the Alleghany mountains. It is also common in the northern part of the Mississippi valley. It is, when full grown, a large and lofty tree, growing principally in deep, cool soils. In some localities it is quite abundant, and, when sawed into boards, is much used as a substitute for Pine or Tulip Tree wood. The wood is light, soft and of little durability, but is nevertheless valuable for many purposes. Bees are fond of the flowers, and gather from them abundance of honey of the very best quality. The bark is also an article of some importance. It is peeled from the trees in June, and soaked in running water two or three weeks, or till the inner part will divide easily into thin layers; the outside bark is then taken off, and the inner part laid by for use. It is much employed by nurserymen and gardeners in budding, grafting and tying up vines and small packages.

The Linden is one of those trees which are not valuable for timber until they have attained a considerable size. Although less deserving extensive propagation than several other forest trees, it yet has useful properties which recommend it for planting to a limited extent. It is often planted for shade, and is esteemed for that purpose. It produces seed in considerable quantity, which, if sown when ripe, or kept in damp sand till spring, will mostly germinate the first season. The seedlings transplant easily. It is also propagated by layers.

2. *Tilia heterophylla* — *White Linden.*

Leaves, smooth, and bright green above, silvery, whitened with a fine down underneath.

This species, which is not found so far north as the preceding, is by some considered a variety of it, and differs principally in the greater size of its leaves and flowers, and the inferior magnitude of the tree. The qualities of the wood and bark are the same as in the preceding species. As an ornamental tree it is considered superior. Meehan says that the most common Weeping Linden of the nurseries is of this species. It is propagated like the preceding.

3. *Tilia Europea—European Linden.*

Leaves, cordate, acuminate, serrate, smooth beneath, twice the length of the petioles; petals without scales.

The European Linden, like the American, is a tree of large size. It has been much planted for shade in and around cities in the Atlantic States. Its leaves are smaller, and its foliage more dense than in the American tree, but it is apt to cast its leaves very early in autumn. It does not appear to thrive in the soil of the Illinois prairies. The wood resembles that of the American species, and the imported bass matting is made from the bark. It is propagated principally by layers.

ULMUS—ELM.

Natural Order, Urticaceæ.

Calyx, bell-shaped, four to nine-cleft; stamens, four to nine; ovary, flat, two-celled; styles, two; fruit, one-celled, one-seeded, winged all round.

There are several species of Elm, of which four are natives of America. They are long-lived trees, and most of them are of large size. Some of them are valued for their timber, and nearly all are fine ornamental trees. All the species produce their flowers before the leaves, and ripen their seeds in spring, usually in the latter part of May. The seeds are light, and, being surrounded by a membraneous wing, are widely scattered by the wind. They should be sown as soon as practicable after ripening. If the season be favorable, the young trees will grow to the height of a foot or more the first year. Should the weather be hot and dry, the young plants must be shaded from the sun at their first appearance. They should not be allowed to remain in the seed-bed more than two years. Elms can be transplanted as successfully as most other trees.

1. *Ulmus Americana*—*White Elm.*

Buds and branchlets smooth; branches not corky; leaves, obovate-oblong or oval, abruptly pointed, sharply and often doubly serrate; flowers, in close fascicles; calyx, seven to nine-lobed; fruit smooth, except the margin.

The White Elm is called by Michaux, "the most magnificent vegetable of the temperate zone." In many parts of the United States it is the most popular shade tree. It is one of the largest deciduous trees of North America; and combines gracefulness, beauty and majesty in a greater degree than almost any other. No tree is more popular for planting in avenues, parks, and in the streets of towns and villages. It is long-lived, of rapid growth, and endures the dust and smoke of large towns better than most other trees. Growing in the forest, it often reaches the height of eighty or one hundred feet; but its beauty and gracefulness are never fully developed when crowded among other trees.

The White Elm is most commonly found along the banks of rivers, and in moist and substantial soils. It will, however, thrive in dry land, but not in that which is very sterile. The wood is employed for the naves of wheels, the panels of carriages, and various other purposes; but as it is not durable, and warps badly when sawed into lumber, it is little esteemed, and seldom used when better timber can be obtained. Its cultivation can be recommended only for ornamental purposes.

2. *Ulmus racemosa—Corky White Elm.*

Leaves, nearly as in the preceding; bud scales, downy-ciliate and somewhat pubescent, as are the young branchlets; branches often with corky ridges; flowers, racemed.

This species, which greatly resembles the White Elm, like that becomes a large tree, and is frequently confounded with it. It grows principally in the neighborhood of streams, and is sometimes called River Elm. The wood is tougher and finer grained than that of the White Elm. It is most readily distinguished by the corky ridges on the branches.

3. *Ulmus alata—Wahoo, Winged Elm.*

Leaves, small, ovate-oblong, and oblong-lanceolate, acute; bud scales, nearly smooth; branches, corky-winged.

The Wahoo grows in low lands in the Southern States, and is found as far north as Southern Illinois. It is a handsome tree, rarely exceeding thirty or forty feet in height. It is readily distinguished by the conspicuous corky ridges on opposite sides of the branches. The wood is said to be fine-grained and valuable, but the tree is not sufficiently common for extensive use. It is preferred for the naves of carriage wheels.

4. *Ulmus fulva—Red Elm, Slippery Elm.*

Leaves, ovate-oblong, taper-pointed, doubly serrate, rough above, soft, downy beneath; buds, soft, downy before expansion, with rusty hairs; branchlets, downy.

The Red Elm is a middle-sized tree, seldom exceeding fifty or sixty feet in height, and two feet in diameter. It is much more common in the Western than in the Atlantic States. Fuller speaks of it as growing in low grounds, and Meehan says it will thrive in low, wet soil, where the other Elms will not. According to my own observation, which has not been very limited, it is usually found on drier lands, and in more elevated situations, than the other native species.

The Red Elm is not so graceful as the White Elm, and is less esteemed as an ornamental tree. On the other hand, the wood is held in higher estimation.

It is of better quality than that of the White Elm, stronger, and more durable when exposed to the weather. The small trees are extensively used for the hubs of carriage and wagon wheels, not being liable to crack open in seasoning, and holding the spokes firmly. The proportion of sap-wood in the Red Elm is very small. Some have recommended its use for posts, but I have not found it durable when employed for that purpose. It lasts a long time when used for rails, but soon decays when in contact with the earth. On the whole, its timber is of sufficient value to justify its preservation and increase.

5. *Ulmus campestris—English Elm.*

Leaves, doubly serrate, rough; flowers, nearly sessile, four-cleft; fruit, oblong, deeply cloven, smooth.

The English Elm is a large and long-lived tree. It was long since introduced, and trees of considerable size are to be met with in the Atlantic States. Michaux says that in his time there were Elms in France twenty-five or thirty feet in circumference, and eighty or ninety feet high. Meehan calls it a finer ornamental tree than the White Elm, but it is difficult to perceive in what respect it is so. As a timber tree, it is doubtless of very extensive utility. Michaux speaks of it as one of the most useful trees in the mechanic arts on the Eastern Continent, and recommends its culture in the United States in preference to any of the native Elms. The wood is said to be most valuable when grown in dry, strong, soils.

The tree is of stiffer and more upright habit of growth than the White Elm, and is one of the most pestilent producers of suckers known; lawns, where it is planted, becoming literally filled with them. This would not be an objection to it as a forest tree. Loudon remarks that it rarely produces seed, and is commonly propagated by suckers, layers, and grafting. It was cultivated by the ancients, and the varieties are numerous.

6. *Ulmus montana—Scotch Elm, Witch Elm.*

Leaves, pointed, rough, broad, and doubly serrate; flowers on longish peduncles, loosely tufted, five to six-cleft; fruit, rhomboid-oblong, slightly cloven, naked.

This species has larger and darker-colored foliage than the English Elm, and is of more vigorous growth. Its wood, although considerably used in Great Britain, is looked upon as inferior to that of the English Elm. As it does not produce suckers from its roots, it is to be preferred as an ornamental tree, and it is only for this purpose that it merits notice. It is a large, handsome tree.

CHAPTER XIII.

CONIFEROUS TREES.

The Conifers (cone-bearing trees), constitute a very large proportion of the forests of North America. Large tracts of the British Provinces, and of the northern parts of the United States—of the ridges of the Alleghanies—of the summits and sides of the Rocky Mountains, and of the country west to the Pacific Ocean, are covered with them. In the maritime parts of the southern Atlantic States—in the greater part of Florida, and extensive tracts in the States bordering on the Gulf of Mexico, Pines constitute the principal growth of wood. The family of Conifers comprises some of the most valuable kinds of timber known. The evergreen forests of the United States have unquestionably contributed more to their wealth and advancement than the richest mines of gold and silver could have done. At least nine-tenths of the wood sawed into lumber and consumed in the country, is the product of resinous trees. The greater part of the woodwork of buildings of every sort is of this description, and immense quantities are employed in fencing the treeless plains of the Mississippi valley. The demand is increasing, and it is a matter worthy the serious consideration of all thinking men how the supply of an article of such prime necessity is to be continued. As fast as the government lands are offered for sale, the valuable tracts of Pine timber are monopolized by speculators, who, regardless of every consideration but immediate profit, hasten to pocket the proceeds. Intelligent Europeans regard with astonishment the reckless and almost wanton destruction of the trees in the forest, the loss by carelessness in the transportation, and the wastefulness in the manufacture. The concentration of the Pine forests in fewer hands must, of course, rapidly enhance the price of lumber. As has already been said, the Pine forests of the Northwestern States are likely to fail in less than twenty-five years; those of New York are wholly exhausted, and those of Maine nearly so. In both these States, Spruce and Hemlock are largely substituted, but even this resource must ere long fail, and the ravages of fire, and the influx of settlers will to a great extent check, if not wholly prevent, the reproduction of the forests. Fortunate will it be if the owners of the soil can be aroused to adopt an efficient system of forest planting in time to prevent the evils and privations sure to accompany a general scarcity of timber.

Most of the more valuable kinds of Conifers will thrive upon thin and unproductive soils, or in situations too broken and rocky for cultivation. Thousands of farms in all parts of the country have more or less land of this description, which might be profitably devoted to growing Pine, Larch, or Spruce timber. Such plantations would add greatly to the value of any farm, and ensure it a more ready sale in case the proprietor should wish to dispose of it.

With few exceptions, the Conifers are not valuable for use until they have attained a considerable size. Such is the case with the Pines, the Hemlock, and in a less degree, the Spruces. Few who plant them can expect to realize the full profit of the enterprise. Probably forty or fifty years would elapse before they would be large enough to be manufactured into lumber. Still, the advantages derived from shelter, and the use of the small trees thinned from the plantation, would not be trifling.

As has previously been asserted, evergreens make the best screens for shelter, affording efficient protection at the season when it is most needed. The advantages of such shelter for dwellings and outhouses have been already set forth. Nor should the ornamental character of evergreens be unnoticed. Planted with proper regard to arrangement, in belts, clumps, or singly around a habitation, they give cheerfulness to the landscape when all other trees are leafless, and constitute a means of beauty and adornment which no person of taste can fail to appreciate. On the other hand, for nearly half the year few dwellings of civilized men appear more desolate and uninviting than many on the open prairies of the West, that have for years been occupied without an attempt to plant an evergreen, or ornamental tree of any kind, to vary the cheerless monotony of the landscape, or a screen to check the bleak winds that come sweeping for many miles over drifting snows. There is, however, evidently, a growing disposition in the community to plant trees. Good example is not without its influence, and there is reason to hope that the improvement, although gradual, will be progressive and permanent.

One fact in relation to Coniferous trees I have never seen noticed in any publication, viz.: that they will not endure the smoke and soot from bituminous coal. When they are exposed to its influence, the foliage is first blackened, the leaves gradually die and drop off. The trees of course become unsightly objects, and eventually perish. It is consequently useless to plant them in compactly built towns or villages where that kind of coal is largely employed as fuel.

CHAPTER XIV.

PROPAGATION OF CONIFERS FROM SEED.

In the climate of the United States, so much skill and care are necessary in raising Coniferous trees from seed, that a separate article is required for its consideration. The method described below is mainly that practiced by Robert Douglas, of Waukegan, Illinois, the most extensive and successful grower of seedling conifers in America, who, with great kindness and liberality, has explained to me his mode of operation, and furnished much valuable information which could hardly have been obtained elsewhere.

The soil most suitable for raising Conifers from seed, is a light, sandy loam, which should be prepared as finely as possible. A soil that is tenacious should have its surface well mixed with sand or vegetable mould. Beds are then laid out, four feet wide, with a space of one foot between. These beds are slightly raised in the middle, the sides being but little higher than the alleys, and are raked quite smooth and fine. Along the sides of the beds, stakes are driven at convenient distances, to which narrow boards are nailed, raising them three or four inches above the surface of the ground, to allow a free circulation of air underneath. These boards serve to support the screen, which is made of laths with a piece of lath nailed across each end. The laths are placed about one and a half inches apart, not more. The seed is sown broadcast, and raked in. The raking-in is an operation requiring some skill and judgment, and is not to be trusted to a clumsy, awkward hand. After sowing, if the ground be somewhat dry, a light roller is passed over it, or a piece of a board with a handle attached, is pressed upon the surface. Some recommend a covering of fine sand or vegetable mould, not to exceed a quarter of an inch in thickness. When the sowing is completed, the screen is put upon the frame. This, in case of dry weather, will aid in keeping the surface of the beds moist until the seeds come up, which is a matter of importance.

Another sort of screen is at present principally used by Mr. Douglas, not for its superiority or greater cheapness, but on account of the difficulty of procuring laths in sufficient quantities at wholesale prices. Rows of posts seven feet high are set ten feet apart, and eight feet distant in the rows. Fence boards, six inches wide and sixteen feet long, are nailed upon these at the top. Slender poles are laid across, and on these are placed bushes and branches of trees with the leaves on them. This sort of screen is constructed the summer previous to sowing. The beds are so laid out that each row of posts is in the middle of a bed. If the soil is tenacious, it is best to throw it up in ridges the fall previous to sowing, that it may pulverize more easily in the spring.

The seeds are sown pretty thickly. A pound of seed of the Norway Spruce occupies about twenty-five feet in length of a bed four feet wide. The extent of surface appropriated to other kinds is regulated to some extent by the number of seeds in a pound, as noted in the table to be given hereafter. The European Larch is sown more thickly, one-fourth to two-thirds of the seeds being worthless.

Mice are great devourers of the seeds of the Conifers. It is sometimes necessary to set traps for them, and everything in the neighborhood of the seed-beds likely to harbor them should be removed. Some kinds of birds are very fond of the seeds, and will collect in numbers upon the beds if unprotected, and do a great deal of mischief. A light covering of straw or evergreen branches will protect the seeds from the birds, and I have found a mulching with leaves of the White Pine to stop the ravages of mice. All such coverings should be carefully taken off when the young plants begin to appear. According to Loudon, the seeds of most kinds of Conifers will come up in from thirty to fifty days after sowing. Those of the Larch are more tardy in vegetating than the Norway Spruce or Scotch Pine. Fresh seed should always be used; that which is old is commonly of little value. Larch seed loses its vitality in less than a year after being extracted from the cones.

The critical period for young evergreens is the first two or three months after their appearance. If they can be carried safely through the first summer, there is not much difficulty in managing them afterwards. They are easily scorched by the rays of the sun, so that it is absolutely necessary to protect them during the hot weather. In the climate of America, what is called *damping off* is perhaps the greatest difficulty to contend with. This is the rotting of the stem at the surface of the ground, which, if not checked, will in some seasons destroy the greater part of the plants. It usually occurs while the plants are in the seed-leaf, and appears to be caused by a combination of heat with too much moisture. It was scarcely seen in the dry summer of 1870. The usual remedy is the liberal application of dry sand, scattered with the hand or from a fine sieve. The sand should be kept at hand ready for use. This disease appears more likely to occur on rich soils than on those that are poor. Young plants of most species grow slowly the first two or three years; but some few, such as the Gray and Scotch Pines, and the Larch, are comparatively rapid in their growth.

Late in autumn the young plants receive a light covering of leaves, on which is placed straw or small branches in sufficient quantity to prevent their being blown off by the wind. This will secure the plants from being drawn out of the ground by frequent thawing and freezing. Straw or marsh hay will answer, if leaves are not to be had.

In removing the plants from the seed bed, the strongest are taken out the first or second year, according to their vigor of growth, and the weaker are allowed to remain another year. Larches are almost uniformly thinned the first year, and are all removed the second year.

It may be proper here to remark, that so much care and skill are requisite to raise Conifers from seed, and the uncertainty of success on the part of a novice so great, that it is cheaper for planters generally to buy of those who make their propagation a business, than to attempt to grow them themselves.

The following table, for which I am under obligations to Mr. R. Douglas, shows the number of seeds in a pound of twenty species of Coniferous trees. It was the result of several weighings of each kind, and the variation was very trifling, except in the Larch and Pear seeds. One-fourth to two-thirds of Larch seeds are abortive, and the more perfect the seeds the fewer in a pound.

Abies Nordmanniana, Nordmann's Fir	8,000
Abies pectinata, Common Silver Fir -	8,000
Abies pichta, Siberian Silver Fir - -	40,000
Abies Fraseri, Fraser's Balsam Fir -	45,000
Abies Canadensis, Hemlock Spruce -	100,000
Abies balsamea, Balsam Fir - -	33,000
Abies excelsa, Norway Spruce - -	58,000
Abies alba, White Spruce - - -	160,000
Cedrus Atlantica, African Cedar - -	7,000
Pinus Cembra, Cembran Pine - -	2,700
Pinus strobus, White Pine - - -	20,000
Pinus Austriaca, Austrian Pine -	28,000
Pinus sylvestris, Scotch Pine - -	69,000

Pinus laricio, Corsican Pine - -	33,000
Pinus rigida, Pitch Pine - - -	66,000
Pinus Mugho, Mugho Pine - -	70,000
Pinus Pinaster, Seaside Pine - -	12,000
Lurix Europea, European Larch 60 to	75,000
Thuja occidentalis, American Arbor Vitæ	320,000
Biota orientalis, Chinese Arbor Vitæ	33,000
Pear seeds - - - - - 12 to	15,000
Apple seeds - - - - -	12,000

Abies Canadensis—Canadian Hemlock Spruce.

CHAPTER XV.

TRANSPLANTING CONIFERS.

In Europe, plantations of Pine and Spruce are sometimes made on a large scale, by sowing the seed either in drills or broadcast where the trees are finally to remain. This is not generally the most profitable mode, and is not likely to be practiced in this country. A great quantity of seed is required, and there are other objections. Undoubtedly, the most eligible method is to plant young trees of proper size, grown in a nursery.

The Conifers require greater care in transplanting than deciduous trees. Every one knows that the latter suffer more by removal when in leaf, than after the leaves have fallen. It is not claimed that evergreens suffer in like degree, but they will by no means endure the same exposure in transplanting at the ordinary season. When taken up, their roots should be carefully prevented from becoming dry, and guarded from all exposure to sun and wind until they are again placed in the earth. Many evergreens perish from the want of proper precaution in this

15

respect. The roots should be plunged into a mixture of loam and water, so as to coat them with mud, immediately after taking up. In planting trees that are not small, the roots should be extended on all sides to their full length, and care should be taken that no vacancies are left among the roots unfilled with earth. Plenty of water thrown into the pit when partially filled, will pack the earth closely about the roots. Trees should be planted no deeper than they formerly grew. The earth should be trodden firmly over the roots, and no water applied after the planting is finished. A thick mulching of rotten chips, or some kind of litter is very beneficial in case of dry weather following the planting. Fresh stable manure should never be used about the trees. Some advise removing large evergreens with a ball of frozen earth around the roots. In practicing this method, the roots of the tree are almost uniformly cut shorter than they need have been if transplanted in the usual way, and as it is mainly the coarser parts of the roots that are inclosed in the ball of earth, the advantage is at least questionable. Damp, cloudy, or wet weather is in all cases the best for transplanting evergreens. A clear, sunshiny day, with a drying wind, is a bad time, and a cold, freezing atmosphere still worse.

The proper time for transplanting Coniferous trees is a matter respecting which there are different opinions. In countries where the ground is never deeply frozen, they may be safely removed at any time in mild weather, when not in a growing state. In colder climates, the latter part of August and first half of September is considered by many the best time. This may do very well when the weather is not too dry, but wouid not be safe in the protracted droughts which frequently occur at that season in the Mississippi valley. Later fall planting is risky in any state of the weather. In the West, spring is generally regarded as the best time. My own opinion is, that is should be done as early as practicable; others favor later planting. It certainly is not safe to defer it until the trees begin to grow. Late planted trees often suffer from the occurrence of hot, dry weather, before they are ready to commence growing.

Young trees, from twelve to eighteen inches high, are quite large enough for use in forming plantations for timber. The plants should be strong and vigorous —not slender in consequence of being grown too thickly. They should be carefully planted, and the earth pressed firmly down upon the roots. They should then receive good cultivation until it is no longer necessary.

As has been previously remarked, Coniferous trees, with a few exceptions, are not very valuable until they have grown to a considerable size. They are manufactured into boards, planks, scantling, and square timber. To make the best lumber, tall, straight trees, of nearly uniform diameter, and free from knots, are necessary. To produce such, they must be thickly grown when young. Trees grown in open situations expend great part of their vigor in the production of side branches; the trunk tapers rapidly from the base, and the wood abounds in knots. When they are closely planted, fewer and smaller side branches are produced, which, as the tree extends rapidly upwards, die and drop off, or may be removed without injury. A plantation may consist entirely of the species which is designed for timber, or, if the young trees be scarce or expensive, they may be planted at such distances that they can be allowed to remain until they are large enough to be of some value, and the intermediate spaces be filled with inferior trees, to be removed as occasion requires. This subject will be more particularly noticed in the consideration of individual species. It may here be repeated that it is of primary importance to prevent the roots of young evergreens from becoming dry while out of the ground. If this be neglected, no subsequent care and attention will avail to save them.

Native evergreens of small size are annually brought in considerable quantities from the forests of the north, and distributed among the nurserymen of more southern latitudes. If they are properly handled, the operation, except in very unfavorable seasons, is attended with considerable success. The most suitable size for removal is from four or five inches to one foot in height. Plants growing in the most open situations are in all cases to be preferred. They should be dug up—not pulled—and the roots immediately secured from exposure by covering them with damp moss. When packed for transportation, damp moss should be freely used about the roots, and openings made in the top and sides of the box, with spaces through the middle sufficient to give free ventilation, and prevent heating. When they reach their destination, they should be immediately taken from the box and carefully bedded in a shady place until planted. In planting, the soil should be deeply stirred and made mellow, and the plants set very thickly in beds, first dipping the roots in thin mud. They should then, without delay, be thickly shaded by placing a screen two or three feet above them. This may be made of branches, with the leaves on them, or if these be wanting, of brush and straw over it. When the weather becomes cool, in autumn, the screen should be removed. If allowed to remain through the winter, it becomes a skulking place for rabbits, who will be likely to do great mischief by biting off the young trees. Two years is a proper time for the plants to remain in the bed, after which they should be planted in nursery rows.

Pruning.

Coniferous trees grown singly, or in groups for ornament, seldom need pruning. Irregular side branches sometimes require shortening, and if two or more leading shoots are thrown out, as will sometimes happen, all but the most vigorous one should be cut out. When the leader is lost, it may be restored by lashing a rod to the stem of the tree, and tying one of the side shoots to it, in a position as nearly upright as possible. The lower branches of trees grown thickly in timber plantations soon die of themselves, and should be cut off close to the trunk. If this be neglected, and the dead branches remain a considerable time, the stumps become buried in the wood of the trunk, to the great injury of the timber. This is particularly true of the Larch. As a general rule, two-thirds of the height of a tree designed for timber should be destitute of branches.

When evergreens several feet in height are transplanted, the operation is more likely to be successful if the side branches are shortened. Especially is this the case with the Red Cedar.

CHAPTER XVI.

INDIVIDUAL CONIFEROUS TREES.

The family of the Coniferæ includes thirty or forty genera, and a great number of species. Many of them are wholly unsuited to the climate of the northern part of the United States, and a still larger proportion are fit only for amateur culture. The Conifers of the States on the Pacific coast comprise some of the most magnificent productions of the vegetable creation. Very few of them, however, can be successfully cultivated in corresponding latitudes east of the Rocky Mountains, and all are as yet too scarce and too expensive to admit of any but very limited culture. In the present work, the descriptions will be confined, principally, to well known native species, with some of foreign origin. Those who may desire a more extended account of this class of trees are referred to Hoopes' Book of Evergreens, the most complete treatise on the subject hitherto published in this country.

NATURAL ORDER, CONIFERÆ.

Sub Order, Abietineæ.

ABIES—SPRUCE, FIR.

Leaves, scattered, short, sometimes two-ranked; sterile catkins, scattered or clustered towards the ends of the branches; fertile catkins, lateral or terminal, on branches of the preceding year; scales of cones, thin, not thickened at the apex, nor with a prickly point; seeds, with a persistent wing.

Among Coniferous trees, the Spruces rank next to the Pines in the usefulness of their timber. Some of the species combine lightness, strength and elasticity in a greater degree than any of the Pines, and are therefore preferred for masts and yards of vessels. The largest and loftiest species are found upon the northwest coast of America.

1. *Abies alba — White Spruce, Single Spruce.*

Leaves erect, slender, scattered, one-half to three-fourths of an inch long; color, light glaucous green; cones, oblong-cylindrical, one to two inches long; edges of the scales entire.

The White Spruce is found in the northern parts of the United States, and northward nearly to the Arctic Ocean. In favorable situations, its ordinary stature does not exceed fifty or sixty feet. It is found in the same localities as the Black Spruce, but in Canada and the United States is much less common than that species. The wood is considered inferior to that of the Black Spruce, but is sawed into lumber and is used for the spars and masts of vessels. It is not esteemed for fuel, as it snaps frequently in burning, like the Chestnut.

This species is a very elegant tree, while young. Its shape is regularly conical, its habit of growth very compact, and the hue of its foliage a lively glaucous green. On old trees, and in poor, dry soils, the foliage is thin and scanty. It is only as an ornamental tree that its cultivation can be recommended. For useful purposes, the Black Spruce and the Norway Spruce are every way superior.

2. *Abies nigra—Black Spruce, Double Spruce.*

Leaves, short, scarcely more than half an inch long, stiff, somewhat appressed to the branches, dark green; cones, ovate, or ovate-oblong, one to one and a half inches long, edge of the scales thin, wavy or notched.

The Black Spruce is indigenous to the colder parts of North America, and is most abundant in the British Provinces and the northeastern parts of the United States. It is found chiefly in swampy lands, in mountain valleys, and wherever the soil is humid, deep and black. In such situations it sometimes constitutes the entire growth of wood. I have seen it growing in masses, the trees varying from a few inches to two feet in diameter, and so thickly crowded that a team of horses could not be driven among them. The smaller trees had a mere tuft of branches on the top. It is found southward, along the summits of the Alleghanies; and the Black Mountain, in South Carolina, is said to derive its name from the dark foliage of this tree.

The Black Spruce grows to the height of seventy or eighty feet, with a diameter seldom exceeding two feet. It is sawed into lumber, and in the regions where it is common, it is largely used as a substitute for the White Pine, which has become scarce. It is tougher than the White Pine, and is more liable to crack in seasoning, but is preferred by many for floors. It is used for the rafters and beams of buildings in preference to the White Pine, being stronger and more durable. It furnishes the best yards and spars for vessels, being considered better for that purpose than the Norway Spruce, but does not grow large enough for the masts of the largest ships. An oil, or "essence," is extracted from the small branches, which is used in the manufacture of Spruce beer.

For ornamental purposes the Black Spruce appears to be generally less esteemed than the White or Norway Spruces. A cool moist atmosphere seems necessary to its full development, and I have seen finer specimens in the wilds of the countries congenial to its growth, than I have ever met with in cultivation. It is most likely that in climates warmer than that in which the Black Spruce naturally grows, the Norway Spruce will be found the most profitable tree for forest culture, particularly as its growth is more rapid.

The cones are shorter than those of the White Spruce, and are often produced in great abundance.

They are ripe at the end of autumn, and must be gathered immediately in order to secure the seeds, as they soon open, and allow them to escape.

The Red Spruce is a variety equally valuable, differing only in the larger and redder cones, and redder bark. Another variety, called by some Blue Spruce, is brought from the forests of Northern Michigan and Wisconsin. The leaves are of a bluish color, slender and loosely spreading, and can scarcely be distinguished from the White Spruce except by the cones. These it often produces when not more than three feet high.

3. *Abies excelsa—Norway Spruce.*

Leaves, scattered, rigid, curved, quadrangular; cones, from five to seven inches long, cylindrical, terminal, pendent; scales, slightly incurved, truncate at the summit; cotyledons, seven to nine; seeds, small, with a long wing.

The Norway Spruce is the loftiest tree of the European forests, growing to the height of from one hundred and twenty to one hundred and fifty feet, and sometimes even more. The trunk is uniformly straight and upright with a diameter of from two to five feet. According to Michaux it is one hundred years in attaining its full growth. It is indigenous to the northern parts of Europe and Asia, but in more southern countries, abounds only among the mountains. On the Alps of Switzerland, it is often found about one hundred and fifty feet in height, growing on moist soils in mountain valleys, with hard, tough, and very durable timber. In Lapland and Siberia, it is found growing further north, and at a greater elevation than any other tree except the Birch, which is sufficient evidence of its hardiness.

The wood of the Norway Spruce is strong, light and elastic; and varies in durability according to the soil upon which it was grown. The least valuable timber is said to be produced on light, poor soils, in elevated situations. The trees are sawed into planks and boards which, under the name of White Deal, are employed for the same purposes as the White Pine in this country. The smaller trees are imported to Great Britain from Norway in the form of entire trunks, from thirty to sixty feet long, and not more than six or eight inches in diameter at the thickest end. Loudon remarks: "The young trees, especially when the bark is kept on, are found to be more durable than any other species of Pine or Fir, with the single exception of the Larch; and for this reason they are admirably adapted for fencing, for forming roofs to agricultural buildings, and for a variety of other purposes." The bark is used for tanning leather, and the resin is the Burgundy pitch of commerce.

With regard to the merits of this tree for ornamental purposes, opinions differ widely. Some object to the stiffness and formality of its appearance, and consider its regular form a defect. It is nevertheless generally popular in the United States. A well grown tree, standing alone upon a lawn and clothed with branches to the ground, is to most people an object of admiration. Many persons plant trees without appear-

Screen of Norway Spruce.

ing to consider that they will ever require room for development. I have repeatedly seen three or four Norway Spruces growing on a cemetery lot twenty feet square.

Whatever opinion may be entertained respecting its ornamental character, there can be no doubt that the Norway Spruce is pre-eminently fitted for plantations designed for shelter. In the discussions of the Horticultural Societies of Illinois, the advantages of evergreen belts for the protection of orchards, of houses and farm buildings, have been for years persistently pressed upon the attention of cultivators of the soil. The Norway Spruce has been designated as the most suitable tree for this purpose. No other evergreen is more easily raised from seed, no other is more cheaply obtained from nurseries—no other is more successfully transplanted. It is perfectly hardy, its growth is vigorous and rapid, its branches and foliage dense and compact, and it readily adapts itself to a variety of soils and climates. Its lower branches are persistent, its growth is perfectly upright, and where room is allowed it pushes its limbs out on all sides in defiance of the force of the winds.

Although the timber of the Black Spruce is in some, perhaps most respects equal to that of the Norway Spruce, yet the latter is much the most rapid grower; it ultimately attains a much greater size, and more easily accommodates itself to different soils and situations. These considerations seem to render it the more eligible tree for forest culture even in those regions where the Black Spruce naturally grows.

The cones of the Norway Spruce are ripe about the end of November. To obtain the seed they may be gathered at that time and spread in the sun, placed in a warm room, or slightly dried on a kiln, after which the seeds easily drop out. According to Loudon, fifteen gallons of cones will produce two pounds of seeds with the wings on, or twenty ounces without them. The young plants seldom rise more than two inches the first year from the seed. The second year they grow somewhat faster, and the third year put out side branches. The fourth and fifth years they begin to grow fast, putting out branches in whorls.

When this tree is planted in a single row for a screen, six feet between the trees is a proper distance. If two or more rows are planted, ten feet is not too much, setting the trees in each row opposite the spaces between the trees in the next. In planting screens, if they are made broader in some parts than in others, or if detached trees are set on their skirts, it will vary the outline, render their appearance less formal, and produce a better effect.

When plantations, designed for timber, are formed of the Norway Spruce, the young trees may be set four feet apart each way. At this distance they will grow to such a size that the thinnings will be useful for many purposes. If the thinnings are not needed a less expensive way will be to set the trees eight feet apart, and plant the intervening rows and spaces with corn or potatoes. After two years of culture, the young trees will be well established, and the vacancies may then be filled with slips of Lombardy Poplar,

White Willow, or Golden Willow, set two feet apart in the rows. The cultivation should be continued until the whole are growing vigorously. The Poplars or Willows are to be thinned as occasion requires. If the trees are planted as indicated in the accompanying diagram, the Spruces will be about nine feet apart; they will be evenly distributed, and will have room to grow to such a size as to be of some value for timber before it will be necessary to thin them.

```
* . . . * . . . * . . . * . .
. . . . . . . . . . . . . . .
. . * . . . * . . . * . . . *
```

The stars show the position of the Norway Spruces, the dots of the intermediate planting. At this distance six hundred and forty trees may be grown upon an acre. Deciduous trees, which throw out stiff horizontal branches, like the Silver Maple, should not be planted among evergreens, as they are likely to interfere with and injure their leading shoots.

4. *Abies Canadensis—Hemlock, Hemlock Spruce.*

Leaves, one-half of an inch long, flat, linear, obtuse, dark green above, glaucous beneath; cones, three-quarters of an inch long, oval with few scales; branchlets slender, drooping.

The Hemlock is natural to the British Provinces of North America and to the coldest parts of the United States. It is found from the Atlantic to the Pacific Ocean; and as far north as Hudson Bay. In Virginia and North Carolina it grows only on the most elevated ridges, and in the coldest exposures of the Alleghany Mountains. In the soils and climates which best suit it, it is extensively multiplied; and constitutes a large proportion of the evergreen forests in the regions where it grows. When full grown it is seventy or eighty feet in height, with a trunk of nearly uniform diameter for two-thirds of its length; but it often reaches the height of one hundred feet or more. It grows in lighter and dryer soils than the Black Spruce, but very dry situations do not suit it.

The wood of the Hemlock is coarse in its texture, and not very durable; but it is stronger than the White Pine, gives a better hold to nails, and for rough work generally is equally serviceable. It is extensively substituted for the White Pine where the latter has become scarce; and it is to be regretted that economy in this respect is not more regarded in the Western States. For joists, rafters and beams—for the sheathing of roofs, and the sides of wooden houses it is preferable to Pine. As the cost of manufacture and transportation is as great as that of White Pine, and its value in market less, it is not likely to be much used while Pine is abundant.

According to Michaux, the grain of the wood is so oblique, or rather spiral, that it makes the circuit of the tree in ascending a few feet. It is true that this is sometimes the case, as it is in the Oak and other kinds of timber; but as far as my own observation extends, it is only of occasional occurrence, and cannot be cited as an objection to the species generally.

The bark of the Hemlock is valuable for tanning leather; a quality which has unfortunately occasioned a great waste of the timber. Immense numbers of the trees have been felled, stripped of their bark, and left to rot upon the ground.

Although despised as "common" by many in the countries where it is native, the Hemlock has few if any equals among evergreens as an ornamental tree. Meehan says, "It would not be exaggeration to pronounce this the most beautiful evergreen in cultivation." Its branches are slender, graceful and drooping, without the formal arrangement common to the Pines and Spruces. As a screen or ornamental hedge it is far superior to the Red Cedar; it bears clipping well, its foliage is dense, and retains its dark green color in all seasons.

The Hemlock has been considered by many a very difficult tree to transplant. When removed at once from its native forests to open grounds and warmer climates, it is very likely to perish; but after two or more years of culture in the nursery, I have uniformly found it as successfully transplanted as any other evergreen. It is sometimes winter killed on heavy clays, although perfectly hardy on suitable soils.

The cultivation of the Hemlock for timber cannot be recommended. Care should indeed be taken to preserve forests of young trees already established; but for artificial plantations, the Norway Spruce, the White, Red, and Scotch Pines are far more eligible, as their growth is more rapid and their timber more valuable.

5. *Abies balsamea*—*Balsam Fir.*

Leaves, narrowly linear, three-quarters to one inch long, silvery beneath; bark, smooth, with resinous vesicles; cones, three to four inches long, cylindrical, violet-colored, erect; the bracts obovate, serrulate, pointed.

This tree is a native of the coldest parts of the United States and of the British possessions. Its ordinary height does not exceed forty feet, with a diameter of twelve or fifteen inches. The trunk tapers rapidly from the base upwards. In some localities it is said to attain a much greater size, and to equal the Black Spruce in height. The wood is white, soft and deficient in strength. It is often used for the timbers of buildings, but is not often sawed into lumber, from the rarity of stocks of sufficient size. The resin is deposited in vesicles or blisters on the trunk and branches, and is collected and used for medicinal purposes.

The Balsam Fir is very generally popular as an ornamental tree, and it is certainly beautiful while young and vigorous. Some denounce it as short lived and apt to become meagre and decrepid. This is doubtless the case in poor, gravelly and shallow soils; but wherever planted in the deep loam of the Western prairies, (and there are trees there forty feet high) it has thus far retained its full vigor and beauty.

6. *Abies Fraseri—Fraser's Fir, Double Balsam Fir.*

Cones, small, oblong-ovate; the bracts oblong, wedge-shaped, short pointed, the upper part much projecting and reflexed.

Fraser's Fir is found from the western part of New England southward on the highest parts of the Alleghany Mountains. It much resembles the common kind, but is a much smaller tree with shorter and more numerous leaves, and smaller cones. It is perfectly hardy, but has no advantages over the preceding species, and is by many considered inferior.

Abies pectinata (European Silver Fir), was introduced a number of years since, and widely distributed; but as far as my experience and observation have extended, its cultivation has in most cases been quite unsatisfactory.

A. Nordmanniana (Nordmann's Fir), and *A. pichta* (Siberian Silver Fir), are said to be quite hardy, but are not yet common. Some of the California trees are the largest of this genus, and some of them the most beautiful, but they are not hardy in most of the Northern States.

LARIX—LARCH.

Catkins, lateral and scattered, bud-like; sterile flowers, consisting of numerous stamens, inserted on the axis, the pollen of simple spherical grains; cones, ovoid, erect, the bracts and scales persistent; leaves, deciduous, soft, all foliaceous, the primary ones scattered, the secondary very many in a fascicle, developed in early spring from lateral scaly and globular buds; fertile catkins, crimson or red in flower.

The Larches are not evergreen, like most other Coniferous trees, but receive similar treatment in growing from seed, and in subsequent culture. Only two species are common in cultivation in this country. Two more are found west of the Rocky Mountains, and four or five in Asia, but they are as yet little known. All are natives of cold or mountainous countries.

1. *Larix Americana—Black Larch, Hackmatack, Tamarack.*

Leaves, almost thread-form, light bluish-green color; cones, small, ovoid, of few rounded scales; seeds, very small, with short wings.

According to Michaux, this tree, in primitive forests, grows to the height of eighty or one hundred feet, with a straight, slender trunk two or three feet in diameter. The branches are numerous, but seldom large. In Newfoundland and around Hudson's Bay, it grows on the uplands, but within the limits of the United States it is found only in swamps. In cultivation it will thrive in most soils, and grows rapidly on the rich loam of the Western prairies.

Michaux says: "The wood of the American Larch is superior to any species of Pine or Spruce, and unites all the properties which distinguish the European species, being exceedingly strong and singularly durable. In Canada it is considered as among the most valuable timber, and has no fault except its weight." It is certainly very strong, and highly eligible for rafters, and timbers of every description used in building. It is also very durable, when kept from contact with the earth. Some assert that it will last a long time when used for posts. My own experience, which is but limited, is adverse to this opinion, as is also the testimony of many who have been familiar with its use from childhood. Although sometimes used for posts in the countries where it grows, it is little esteemed for that purpose. It has been asserted, and may probably be true, that the Larch timber grown on uplands, far north, is much superior to that grown in swamps, towards its southern limit. It is a handsome ornamental tree, but less so than the European species.

Although the Black Larch is unquestionably inferior to the European Larch in some respects, yet, as has already been stated, it is very valuable for many uses. It flourishes upon the Western prairies—the young plants are cheaply obtained from the swamps of the north—it is of easy culture, and grows rapidly—considerations which should commend it to the attention of tree-planters. The trees should be planted early in spring, before the leaves begin to appear, in rows four feet apart and two to four feet distant in the rows.

It is said that the Black Larch has been sold by vendors as the European Larch, in Iowa, Kansas and Nebraska. Such imposition would be easy when the buyer was not acquainted with the difference between the two kinds, and can only be avoided by purchasing of those who can be depended upon.

2. *Larix Europea—European Larch.*

Leaves, fascicled, linear, soft, one inch long; branches, horizontal, with drooping branchlets; cones, ovate-oblong, one to one and one-quarter inch long, erect; scales, orbicular, reflexed at the margin.

The European Larch rises to the height of from eighty to one hundred feet, and even more, with a proportionate diameter. It is a native of the Alps of France and Switzerland, of the Tyrol, of the Carpathian Mountains, of the Appennines of Italy, and of some places in the south of Russia. It was introduced into England before 1629, but was then spoken of as very rare. A century later it was mentioned by Miller as "pretty common in English gardens." About one hundred years since, the Duke of Athol commenced planting it as a forest tree; and for many years past it has been more extensively cultivated in Great Britain than all other timber trees combined. Ample experience has demonstrated its superior value. Loudon devotes fifty pages of his *Arboretum* to this species alone. As it has been hitherto but little cultivated in America, the testimony in regard to its excellencies is entirely foreign, but there appears to be no reason to suppose that it will prove less valuable here than in Europe.

The European Larch appears to combine the qualities of rapidity of growth, symmetry of form, durability of wood, and adaptability to a variety of uses, in a greater degree than any other timber tree of northern latitudes. Instances can be cited where the Larch, in this country, has reached the height of thirty feet, with a diameter of ten inches, in ten or twelve years from planting. Loudon says: "The rate of growth of the Larch, in the climate of London, is from twenty to twenty-five feet in ten years, from the seed, and nearly as great on the declivities of hills and mountains in the Highlands of Scotland." In Perthshire, Larches of forty-seven years' growth measured thirty inches in diameter, or seven feet ten inches in circumference, at five feet from the ground. "A Larch cut down near Dunkeld, after it had been sixty years planted, was one hundred and ten feet high, and contained one hundred and sixty cubic feet of timber. In a suitable situation, the timber is said to come to perfection in forty years, while that of the Pinaster requires sixty years, and that of the Scotch Pine eighty years." As far as my own observation and experience enable me to judge, the Larch, planted four feet apart each way, may in ten years be grown large enough for fence posts. At that distance, about twenty-seven hundred would grow upon an acre.

The Larch inclines to grow tall, even in open ground. The branches are numerous, but not often large; and when thickly grown, the trunk is straight, clean, and free from knots, and tapers very gradually from the base.

The writers of Europe upon forest trees produce ample evidence of the great durability of the Larch.

Sir Thomas Dick Lauder, quoted by Loudon, observes: "It is unquestionably by much the most enduring timber we have. It is remarkable that whilst the heart wood is not formed at all in other resinous trees till they have lived a good many years, the Larch, on the other hand, begins to make it soon after it is planted; and whilst you may fell a Scotch Pine, thirty years old, and find no heart wood in it, you can scarcely cut down a young Larch large enough to be a walking-stick, without finding just such a proportion of heart wood, compared to its diameter as a tree, as you will find in the largest Larch in the forest, compared to its diameter." The same writer mentions an experiment made in the river Thames: "Posts of equal thickness and strength, some of Larch and others of Oak, were driven down facing the river wall, where they were alternately covered with water by the flow of the tide, and left dry by its fall. This species of alternation is the most trying of all circumstances for the endurance of timber, and accordingly the oaken posts decayed, and were twice renewed, in a very few years, while those made of Larch remained altogether unchanged." A report made by M. Boissel de Monville, on the uses of the Larch, says: "Larch wood is much used in Switzerland for shingles to cover the roofs of the houses, and for vine props. For the latter purpose, it is found the most durable of all kinds of wood; the vine props made of it are never taken up, they remain fixed for an indefinite succession of years, and see crop after crop of vines spring

European Larch.

up, bear their fruit, and perish at their feet, without showing any symptom of decay. In most cases the proprietors of the vineyards are perfectly ignorant of the epoch when these props were first placed there; they received them in their present state from their fathers, and in the same state they will transmit them to their sons. Props made of the Silver Fir, and used in the same soil for the same purpose, would not last more than ten years. In traversing the forests of the Alps, I found frequent proofs of the excellence of the wood of the Larch. The lightning often strikes and shatters these trees, the winds break them, and the effects of time cause them to perish by old age. All these modes of destruction, and many others, made me find a great number of dead and mutilated trees in these forests. Those which were mutilated had not perished on that account. The branches which remained uninjured were still growing with vigor; the heart wood was sound and unchanged, and the trees continued to live during a long series of years. The wood, even of those quite dead, showed no signs of decay, and had evidently remained in the same state a great number of years. I gathered several of the branches, and divided some of the trunks of the dead trees, and though some of the branches were become so brittle as to break easily with the fingers, and the wood of the trunk so dry as to separate into scales, neither showed the least signs of rottenness."

The Larch is the best of timber for rails, fences and out-door fabrics exposed to the weather. It is used in the manufacture of carts, wagons, and implements of husbandry; for the timbers of buildings and for mill work. It makes excellent ties for railroads; and the demand for it for this purpose in Great Britain has caused a heavy draft upon the extensive plantations of Scotland. For hop poles and grape stakes it is better than any other tree. Small trees are said to last longest with the bark on. Larch is as strong as Oak, and more durable; and is considered one of the best kinds of timber for ship building. According to an estimate in Loudon's *Arboretum*, ten acres of Larch will furnish as great an amount of ship timber as seventy-five acres of Oak. Venice turpentine, and Manna de Briançon are produced by the Larch. The bark also is used for tanning.

From the testimony cited above, it appears that there is every encouragement for extensively planting the Larch in this country. Although for some years it will thrive almost anywhere, and become large enough to be useful for farm purposes, yet in some soils and situations it does not ultimately produce valuable timber. Only time and experience can give full information in this respect. In the meantime something may be gathered from European writers. A damp atmosphere is said not to suit the Larch; it does not succeed near the sea, or in the immediate neighborhood of lakes and rivers. It may hence be inferred that the dry atmosphere of the western plains will suit it well. The experience of the Duke of Athol showed that "elevated situations are better for the Larch than low ones—declivities better than flats." There are in all parts of the country river bluffs, steep slopes, bleak, barren hills, or rough, broken lands of little value for any other purpose than timber growing, on which the Larch would thrive. Much of the land planted by the Duke of Athol, was, at the time of planting, worth not more than one shilling per acre. When thirty years old, the trees were thinned to four hundred per acre. The average value of the Duke's plantations, the age ranging from thirty to seventy-two years, was upwards of one thousand pounds sterling per acre.

Probably one of the worst soils for the Larch in the West, would be low, flat land largely composed of vegetable mould, with a retentive subsoil. Such are some of the prairie lands.

In the extensive plantations of Scotland, strong plants of Larch, two years old, and one year transplanted are principally used. Ground sufficiently level for tillage should be prepared and marked out in rows four feet apart; in which the plants may be set three or four feet distant. At three feet, three thousand six hundred plants will be required for an acre. In planting, the earth should be pressed firmly over the roots. Lands too steep or rough for the use of the plough, or declivities where loosening the soil would render it liable to be washed away by rains, may be planted without regard to regularity, further than to place the plants at a proper distance from each other. In such situations a spade or garden trowel may be used in planting. In Scotland a tool not unlike that used by nurserymen, in setting root grafts, is employed for that purpose. With this a slit is made in the ground, the roots of the plant carefully inserted, and the ground trod firmly around them. Care must be taken to keep down all vegetation likely to interfere with the growth of the young trees. Planting must be done early in the spring before the leaves begin to appear. The Larch puts forth its leaves earlier than most other trees, and suffers more than any other by being removed after it has begun to grow.

Unlike evergreen Coniferous trees, both the European and American Larch may be safely planted in autumn. Probably in most places south of latitude 40°, and in many localities north of that parallel, fall planting would be preferable. Especially is it worth trial on the arid plains towards the Rocky Mountains, where fall-planted trees would be in better condition to resist the heat and dryness of the ensuing summer than those set in the spring. The only objection to fall planting is that in certain soils, in some seasons, the young trees are liable to be drawn out of the ground by frosts during the winter. Where this is likely to occur, fall planting had better be avoided. When trees are set in autumn, the soil, if very dry, should be moistened and trod firmly over the roots. Young trees are most likely to be drawn out on level lands, having a retentive subsoil, in seasons when the ground is saturated with moisture.

The Larch, when small, will sometimes take a spreading or straggling form, expending its whole growth in the production of horizontal branches. In such cases it is necessary to prune severely, cutting off all the side branches to force the growth into a strong upright shoot. All side branches of too vigorous growth should be shortened. No other pruning is needed until the trees are ten or twelve feet high; when all dead or sickly limbs should be cut off close to the stem, and others removed at the rate of one, or at most two tiers annually; keeping one-half or two-thirds of the trunk clear of branches. Pruning should be done after the leaves have fallen. In regard to thinning, Loudon says: "Where the object is timber of large size, the trees ought to be thinned out soon after the branches at the lower part of the trunk interfere with one another to such an extent as to destroy all vegetation on the surface of the ground beneath them; but where they are intended for posts, fencing, or other minor country purposes, they ought to be allowed to stand thick so as to be drawn up clean, slender, and straight." The first thinning should be slight, removing only the worthless or least valuable trees. Thinning should be continued until the trees are thirty or thirty-five years old, and the number is reduced to four hundred or five hundred per acre, which is as many as can grow to perfection. The strongest and most vigorous trees should be left, even if the distances between them are not equal. The exercise of judgment and common sense on the part of the cultivator is of more consequence than any rules that can be given.

It has been pretended that the Tyrolese and Scotch Larch are distinct varieties, some claiming that the former is the most valuable, others that the latter is best. There appears to be little if any ground for a distinction. The Larch was originally introduced into Great Britain from the Tyrol and the neighboring mountains of Switzerland, and most of the seed of commerce still comes from these and adjacent countries. The Russian Larch, from the north of Russia and Siberia, is said to be a distinct variety; it was introduced in Scotland by the Duke of Athol on trial, and found to be of little value.

As has previously been remarked, a considerable part of even the best Larch seed sold in market is usually worthless. Whether this arises from its being partially gathered from too young trees, or from a general habit of abortion in fructification, I am unable to determine. Young Larches in this country often produce cones, but as far as my observation extends, the seed is uniformly abortive. Larch seed is sometimes spoiled by the application of too great heat to force the cones to open and discharge their seeds. The seeds retain their vitality but a few months after leaving the cones, and probably old seed is sometimes mixed with fresh, Larch seed is sometimes advertised as "good," forty per cent of which is warranted to grow. Loudon says the cultivators of France and Germany prefer seed from the Valais of Switzerland. Seed from the Tyrol is sold in Scotland at a higher price than that produced there.

The attention of persons in the United States, interested in tree planting, has lately been turned to the Larch, and it is to be hoped that it will ere long be generally and extensively cultivated.

PINUS—PINE.

Flowers monœcious; sterile catkins spiked, formed of numerous stamens on the axis with very short filaments and a scale-like connective; anther cells two, opening lengthwise; fertile catkins solitary or clustered, terminal; fruit a cone, persistent, and formed of woody imbricated scales; seeds nut-like, situated in a hollow at the base of the scales, winged; cotyledons linear, three to twelve; leaves needle-shaped, evergreen, in clusters of two, three or five, with a sheath at the base; blossoms appear in spring, the cones maturing in the autumn of the second year.

The genus Pinus embraces a great number of species, among them some of the most useful trees. These afford excellent material for building; and the greater part of the Pine lumber used in the United States is the product of two species, which, as they are the best, are also the most abundant. Immense quantities of tar, resin, pitch, and turpentine are produced by some species, particularly in the Southern States. Many species are highly esteemed for ornamental purposes. Some of the most elegant are natives of the countries west of the Rocky Mountains; and though many of the trees of that region will not succeed in corresponding latitudes further east, it is probable that some may be found to thrive in the greater part, if not all the sections for which this work is designed.

SECTION QUINEÆ.

FIVE LEAVES IN A SHEATH.

1. *Pinus Strobus—White Pine.*

Leaves, three to four inches long, slender, soft, more or less glaucous, the sheaths deciduous; cones, four to six inches long, cylindrical, drooping, somewhat curved; scales without prickles.

The White Pine is a well known and most useful tree which, in primitive forests, reaches the height of from one hundred to one hundred and sixty feet. It is found throughout the northern parts of the United States, and was formerly very abundant in New England, Northern New York and Pennsylvania. Immense quantities of Pine lumber were, until recently, derived from those regions, and either consumed at home, or shipped to Europe and the West Indies. But now Pine trees of old growth are rare even in the woods of Maine. The scattered specimens which, in long settled parts of the country, were in my youth still to be seen towering far above the surrounding forests, are no longer to be met with. At present, the supply within the limits of the United States is drawn principally from the forests of the Northwestern States.

The value of the wood of the White Pine, and the multiplied uses for which it is employed, are well known. No one of our native forest trees is more generally useful; and no one better merits careful preservation and extensive culture. It is idle to expect a general renewal of the northern forests; the influx of settlers will effectually prevent it; and plantations of Pine will at no remote period be among the most valuable.

The White Pine accommodates itself to a great variety of soils. It grows in poor, sandy or gravelly lands, in rich loams, and in swamps. It will not thrive in a soil composed entirely of sand, nor on lands constantly covered with water. The soil of the Illinois prairies appears to suit it well. On dry uplands its wood is harder, stronger and more resinous than when grown in moister soils; its grain is coarser and the concentric circles more distant. According to Michaux, the wood grown in deep, loose, humid soils, unites in the highest degree the valuable properties for which it is esteemed.

As an ornamental tree, the White Pine is surpassed by few if any of its genus. The formal arrangement of its branches in whorls, which is apparent while it is small, is in thrifty and vigorous trees concealed when they become larger. Its foliage is soft, its hue agreeable, and the whole appearance of the tree graceful. It is indeed looked upon with contempt by some, for the same reason that the Hemlock and other native trees are despised—because it is *so common.*

The wood of the White Pine burns freely, but does not make a lasting fire, nor produce an intense heat. It is not, therefore, particularly valuable until it has reached a size fit for hewing into square timber, or for the manufacture of lumber. Hence, in forming plantations for timber it may be a matter of economy to plant the young trees eight feet apart each way, as directed for the Norway Spruce, and afterwards fill the intermediate spaces with trees of easier propagation and culture, to be cut out as the Pines increase in size. The Lombardy Poplar and White and Golden Willow are best for this purpose. The Silver Maple is less suitable on account of its rigid horizontal branches. The leading shoots of the Pines are very tender while growing, and are easily broken or injured, so that care must be taken that the branches of the other trees do not overtop or in any way interfere with them. After the Pines have reached the height of ten or fifteen feet they may be pruned as directed for the Larch.

The seeds ripen early in autumn, and must be gathered immediately, as the cones open for their release by the first of October, and in some seasons earlier.

2. *Pinus Cembra—Cembran Pine, Stone Pine.*

Leaves, two to three inches long, triangular, dark green; sheaths, deciduous; cones, three inches long, ovate, erect, with obtuse, slightly hooked scales.

The Cembran Pine grows on the Alps, where, in some places, it forms large forests. It is also found in Siberia. It appears to be, ordinarily, a tree of moderate size, although some speak of it as growing very large. The wood is highly esteemed in its native countries. It is soft, very durable, and the grain is so fine as to be scarcely perceptible. It is much used for carving and for the wainscoting of houses. It has an agreeable odor which it retains for many years. The tree is handsome, the growth and foliage are very dense; and it has the merit of thriving in almost all soils and situations. It is perfectly hardy, but its growth is very slow even in rich soils; and this is doubtless the principal reason why it has been so much less known and propagated than other Pines, inferior both in beauty and in the quality of their timber. Where it abounds, the seeds are used for food and oil is extracted from them.

3. *Pinus excelsa—Bhotan Pine.*

Leaves, five to seven inches long, slender, pointed, crowded, glaucous; sheaths, short; cones, six to nine inches long, cylindrical, smooth, pendulous, clustered; scales, broad, thick, wedge-shaped, imbricated; seeds small.

This species greatly resembles the White Pine, and when healthy and vigorous, is even more beautiful. Its leaves are longer, of a brilliant glaucous green color, and its growth is more compact. I have never been able to cultivate it satisfactorily, nor do I know that any one in the State of Illinois has succeeded better. In Northern Illinois the buds are occasionally killed by the winter, but the worst trouble is a blight which sometimes destroys trees six or eight feet high. It is a highly desirable tree, wherever it can be kept in a healthy condition. In its native countries (Nepaul and Bhotan,) it grows to a large size. Its timber is highly esteemed, and is said to resemble that of the White Pine.

P. Lambertiana, P. monticola, P. flexilis, and P. aristata are, according to Hoopes, hardy in the neighborhood of Philadelphia, and merit the attention of amateurs, but are as yet too scarce and too imperfectly tested to be recommended for general culture.

SECTION TERNATIÆ.

THREE LEAVES IN A SHEATH.

4. *Pinus rigida—Pitch Pine.*

Leaves, three to five inches long, rigid, flattened, dark green; sheaths, very short; cones, one to three and a-half inches long, ovoid-conical or ovate, sometimes clustered, persistent; the scales tipped with a short, recurved, stout prickle.

This species of Pine appears to be confined to the States bordering on the Atlantic. I have never heard that it is found west of the Alleghanies. It grows in a variety of soils. In some parts of New England and New York it occupies poor sandy lands, whose barrenness is attested by the meagre, stunted appearance of the trees, which seldom exceed thirty feet in height. Further south it is found on the ridges of the Alleghanies, in better soil and of larger growth. In swamps it attains its greatest size, which is seventy or eighty feet in height, and eighteen to thirty inches in diameter. The sap wood usually comprises three-fourths of the diameter of the tree. The branches are numerous, the wood extremely knotty, and when grown on dry land it is highly resinous and heavy. Where it is abundant and of proper size, lumber of inferior quality is manufactured from it. The wood grown upon low lands is soft and light. The tree abounds in pitch; and before the Revolution considerable quantities of tar and turpentine were collected from it in New England. The wood produces an intense heat in burning, and is used by bakers and brickmakers where it is abundant. Its cultivation for timber cannot be recommended, as there are several species far surpassing it in value; and it is not much esteemed as an ornamental tree.

5. *Pinus Taeda—Loblolly Pine, Oldfield Pine.*

Leaves, six to ten inches long, from elongated sheaths; rigid, light green, slender; cones, oblong; three to five inches long; the scales tipped with short incurved prickles.

The Loblolly Pine is not found north of Virginia, and, probably, will not endure the winters of much higher latitudes. It is a large and lofty tree, growing from fifty to one hundred feet high. The bark is thick, rough and deeply furrowed. It is sometimes called Oldfield Pine, from its disposition to take possession of lands that have been worn out by cultivation and abandoned. On such lands it grows rapidly, although they have been so completely exhausted by mismanagement as to be scarcely capable of producing anything else.

In sections where the Loblolly Pine is abundant, and better timber is not at hand, it is considerably used in the construction of houses. The wood is free from knots, but is of spongy consistence, and is principally composed of alburnum, or sap wood. It shrinks and warps badly, and speedily decays when exposed to the weather. It is one of the least valuable of the Pines for timber, and for ornamental purposes is inferior to many other species of its genus.

6. *Pinus ponderosa—Heavy-wooded Pine.*

Leaves, nine to twelve inches long, broad, twisted, crowded; color, deep green; sheaths, short; cones, three and a-half inches long, ovate, reflexed, clustered; peduncles, short; scales, tipped with a small, sharp, recurved prickle; seeds, with long wings.

This species, from the Pacific coast, is a large tree, very hardy and of rapid growth. The wood is very heavy, and is said to be of great excellence. As far as tested, this tree has succeeded well in the State of Illinois, but, like other species from our western coast, it is not yet common in cultivation.

Pinus australis, the Long-leaved Pine of the Southern States, ranks next to the White Pine in usefulness, but does not come within the limits of this work. P. macrocarpa, P. Sabiniana, and others of this section are as yet imperfectly tested, and not generally known.

SECTION BINÆ.

TWO LEAVES IN A SHEATH.

7. *Pinus sylvestris—Scotch Pine.*

Leaves, twisted, rigid, one and a-half to three inches long; color, light bluish-green; sheaths, short;

cones, ovate-conical; scales, tipped with a retorted spine; seeds, small; cotyledons, five to seven.

The Scotch Pine constitutes a large part of the forests of Sweden, Russia and other countries in the north of Europe. Further south, it is found principally in cold and elevated situations on the Alps, Pyrenees and other mountainous regions. According to Michaux, it is only in cold climates or elevated localities that it arrives at perfection. It reaches the height of eighty feet or more, with a diameter of four or five feet. It is one of the most rapid-growing species of Pine; it thrives in the most dissimilar soils, and is quite at home on barren rocky hills. For general use, it is to the people of Europe what the White Pine is to those of the United States; and, besides, affords great quantities of tar and turpentine. The wood is harder and more resinous than that of the White Pine, and, probably, more durable. Some European writers strongly assert its superiorty to the White Pine for general purposes; a claim which Americans are not disposed to admit. Michaux remarks that they are so different in quality that no comparison can be instituted between them; but he thinks the Scotch Pine superior to the Yellow Pine, which it most resembles.

Young plants of the Scotch Pine are easily procured in quantities, and its cultivation for timber may be unqualifiedly recommended. The excellence of its wood, its rapid growth, its perfect hardiness and its adaptability to different soils are well-established facts. Next to the Larch it is the tree most extensively planted in Great Britain; and there is no doubt that it might be profitably cultivated on waste lands in the northern United States. Its treatment in plantations is the same as that of the White Pine. Plants two or at most three years old are employed for planting. It is very suitable for screens or belts for the protection of orchards or buildings.

In the west, the Scotch Pine has been considerably planted for ornamental purposes; a fact which may be attributed to the limited variety of evergreens in general cultivation, and to the facility with which it is grown. It is inferior in beauty to most of our native species, although in certain situations it shows to good advantage. Michaux remarks that the Scotch Pine bears transplanting with less injury than any other species.

8. *Pinus Austriaca—Austrian Pine.*

Leaves, three to five inches long, rigid, curved towards the twig, sharply pointed; color, dark green; sheaths, short; cones, two to three inches long, slightly curved.

This species is said to be found principally upon the mountains of the Austrian dominions, where it grows to the height of one hundred and twenty feet. In open ground it becomes a spreading tree with stiff, strong branches. In its native countries its timber is much used and highly esteemed. It is strong, tough, and very resinous—makes excellent fuel, and affords great quantities of turpentine.

The Austrian Pine has acquired much popularity, and is generally planted in this country for ornament. It is perfectly hardy in the most northern States, and adapts itself to a variety of soils. Its ornamental character is of that description which appears best at some distance. On close inspection its foliage appears coarse, stiff, and ungraceful; but seen farther off, a well-grown tree standing singly, is a picturesque and agreeable object in a landscape. It is well adapted to the formation of screens or windbreaks, as it grows rapidly, and its strong branches and rigid leaves do not yield readily to the force of the wind. When several feet high it does not transplant so easily as the Scotch Pine, unless it has previously been often removed or root-pruned.

In the West, this species and the Scotch Pine are often greatly injured and sometimes destroyed by the attacks of the Sapsucker (sphyrapicus varius.) The only preventive appears to be powder and shot.

9. *Pinus resinosa—Red Pine.*

Leaves, five to six inches long, semi-cylindrical, dark green, from long sheaths; cones, two inches long, sometimes in large and close clusters; bark, reddish, rather smooth.

The Red Pine, often wrongfully called Norway Pine, grows in the northern parts of the United States and in the British provinces. It is common in the northern parts of Michigan and Wisconsin. It grows in dry sandy soils to the height of seventy or eighty feet, with a diameter of two feet, and a trunk of uniform size for two-thirds of its length. It is said to furnish planks forty teet long without a knot. The wood is heavy, strong, and durable, and for some uses is preferable to the White Pine. It is a beautiful tree, and its vegetation is vigorous and rapid.

This species is one of the most valuable of the Pines, and highly deserves extensive cultivation; but unfortunately it is difficult if not impossible to procure the young trees in considerable quantities. Nine-tenths of the plants brought from the northern forests usually perish in the removal, even though handled with great care. The reason of this is not very obvious, since, after growing two or three years in the nursery, the Red Pine transplants as successfully as other species. Nor is the seed easily obtained. Mr. Robert Douglas informed me that he had offered liberal prices for it without being able to procure any. If some of the cone-gatherers of the European forests could be employed in our northern woods, the seed might undoubtedly be collected. Cones of the Grey Pine containing seed have been sold in Illinois, by knaves, as those of the Red Pine, which they are not very unlike.

The Red Pine is far superior to the Scotch and Austrian Pines for ornamental purposes, and it seems strange that it has not been more generally brought into notice.

10. *Pinus Banksiana—Grey Pine, Scrub Pine.*

Leaves, one to two inches long, oblique, divergent; sheaths, very short; cones, ovate-conical, smooth, often curved; scales, pointless.

This species is found from the northern parts of the United States, nearly to the Arctic Sea; and from Labrador to the valleys of the Rocky Mountains, and the head waters of the Oregon River. It is sometimes met with in Northern Illinois. In Lower Canada and Labrador it is said to be a straggling shrub from three to ten feet high. Dr. Richardson found it in the interior of the continent, twenty to forty feet high, and even more in favorable situations. In Wisconsin, on light sandy soils, it becomes a middle-sized tree. Lapham, Knapp and Crocker, in their report on the Forests of Wisconsin, speak of it as reaching the height of sixty or eighty feet, and furnishing hewed timber thirty or forty feet long and eight inches square. The leaves on vigorous trees are two inches long, and sometimes more. The cones are commonly in pairs, but often single, frequently curved, but as often quite straight. The branches are irregular, long, slender and flexible.

The wood is light, the fibre straight and very tough; but logs are seldom found suitable for sawing into lumber. As fuel, it is equal to any other species of pine, it burns freely and produces great heat. It presents no inducements to propagation as a timber tree.

Notwithstanding the eulogies of Loudon and others, the Grey Pine does not appear to have found much favor for ornamental purposes. It is a handsome tree while young, but when older is disfigured by the persistent cones, which open, become black, and remain on the branches for years. These, and the numerous dead twigs scattered over the interior of the branches, give the trees, while yet healthy and vigorous, the appearance of age and decrepitude. When raised from seed it grows more rapidly for the first few years than any other Pine with which I am acquainted. It transplants easily, even when of considerable size, the roots being numerous and slender.

11. *Pinus inops—Jersey Pine, Scrub Pine.*

Leaves, two to three inches long, rigid, with a short sheath; cones, two to three inches long, oblong-conical, sometimes curved; scales, armed with a straight awl-shaped point.

The Jersey Pine abounds in the Pine barrens of New Jersey, in Maryland and Virginia, and is found in some other States. It grows to the height of from fifteen to thirty feet on poor sandy soils. It is commonly a low, dwarfish tree, with spreading, straggling branches. The wood consists principally of sap, which, with its small size, renders it of little worth. Tar is said to be made from it in Kentucky. On the whole, it appears to be the least valuable of the American Pines. It has never been much propagated or esteemed for ornamental purposes, although it is commended by Meehan and others.

12. *Pinus pungens—Table Mountain Pine.*

Leaves, pale green, two and one-half inches long, stout and stiff, crowded; cones, ovate, sessile, three inches long; scales, armed with strong hooked prickles.

This species is found on the Blue Ridge in Virginia, and southward on the summits of the Alleghany Mountains. It grows to the height of forty or fifty feet, with something of the habit and general appearance of the Scotch Pine, but with more numerous branches. The cones are usually in whorls, and remain on the branches many years. Until lately it has attracted very little attention. It is uncertain how far north it will prove hardy, but it is cultivated by Mr. Douglas at Waukegan, Illinois. In its native localities its timber is not highly esteemed; and as it is not remarkably beautiful, its principal use will probably be to enrich the collection of the amateur.

13. *Pinus mitis—Yellow Pine.*

Leaves, dark green, in pairs, sometimes in threes, three to five inches long, with long sheaths, slender, channeled; cones, oblong-conical or ovoid, two inches long; scales, tipped with a small weak prickle.

The Yellow Pine is extensively diffused throughout the Atlantic States from New England to Florida. In the west it is found in Kentucky, Tennessee and Missouri. It grows sparingly in Southern Illinois, and I have seen small trees among the sand hills at the south end of Lake Michigan. Considerable quantities of lumber of this species were formerly brought to St. Louis from the neighborhood of the Gasconade river, and sold under the name of Gasconade Pine.

The ordinary height of the Yellow Pine is fifty or sixty feet, but in favorable situations it often much exceeds this stature. Its diameter is commonly uniform for two-thirds of its length. It is most abundant in the poorest soils. The timber is very valuable and usually commands a higher price in market than the White Pine. It is highly esteemed in shipbuilding, being used for masts, yards, beams and decks of vessels. Michaux says: "The concentrical circles of the wood are six times as numerous in a given space as those of the Pitch and Loblolly Pines. In trunks fifteen or eighteen inches in diameter, there are only two inches or two and a-half of sap wood, and still less in such as exceed this size. The heart is fine grained and moderately resinous, which renders it compact without great weight. Long experience has proved its excellence and durability. It is considered next in durability to the Long-leaved Pine." From these remarks it would appear that the tree is of slow growth.

The Yellow Pine has been almost entirely neglected in ornamental culture. It is rarely mentioned in nursery catalogues, although superior in beauty to several species in common cultivation To quote Michaux once more: "The Yellow Pine is a beautiful tree, and this advantage it owes to the disposition of its limbs, which are less divergent the higher they are placed upon the stocks, and which are bent towards the body so as to form a summit regularly pyramidical, but not spacious in proportion to the dimensions of the trunk. Its regularity has, perhaps, given rise to the name of Spruce Pine." Meehan and Hoopes also praise its beauty.

If, as Michaux asserts, the Yellow Pine is inferior to the Scotch Pine in the quality of wood, the latter is the more eligible tree for forest culture, as it is of more rapid growth. Still the Yellow Pine merits the attention of tree planters, and preservation where it already exists.

14. *Pinus Laricio—Corsican Pine.*

Leaves, four to six inches long, slender, flexible, very wavy; cones, two to three inches or more in length, oblong-conical; scales, tipped with a very small prickle, often scarcely perceptible; seeds, twice as large as those of the Scotch Pine; cotyledons, six to eight.

This species is a native of the island of Corsica, and other countries in the south of Europe. Its ordinary height is from eighty to one hundred feet. Loudon says: "In the island of Corsica it is said that there are trees of this species from one hundred and forty to one hundred and fifty feet in height." According to the same authority it is a much more rapid grower than the Scotch Pine, but not a long-lived tree; its duration in Corsica being only from seventy to eighty years. The wood is manufactured into valuable lumber, which is easily worked and said to be quite durable. The following instances of its rapid growth are taken from Loudon's *Arboretum*: "The rate of growth in young trees, in the climate of London, is from two feet to three feet a year. A tree in the Horticultural Society's garden, having been twelve years planted, was, in 1834, twenty feet high, and is now (1837) twenty-five feet high. A shoot of the year 1829, with part of 1828, cut from a tree five years old, on M. Vilmorin's estate at Barras, and sent to Mr. Lawson's museum, measured three feet in length, and three and a-half inches in circumference at the thickest end. In the arboretum of Messrs. Loddiges, this species and its varieties had reached the height of from twenty to thirty feet, while the Scotch Pine and its varieties were not above twelve feet. In France, according to Thouin, P. Laricio grows two-thirds faster than the Scotch Pine placed in similar soils and situations."

Hoopes, in his Book of Evergeens, eulogizes this Pine, for ornamental purposes, and remarks that although a native of warm climates, it has in his neighborhood given entire satisfaction. In northern Illinois its hardihood is not well established. I have attempted to cultivate imported plants, but they were injured more or less every winter, and finally perished. Mr. Douglas raises plants from seed, and is of opinion that they will prove more hardy than those brought across the Atlantic. It will. doubtless, succeed in Kansas, southern Illinois and Kentucky; and its rapid growth and valuable timber render its cultivation an object where a speedy result is desired.

Sub-Order—Cupressineæ.

CUPRESSUS—CYPRESS.

Flowers, monœcious on different branches, in terminal small catkins; sterile catkins composed of

Pinus Strobus.

shield-shaped, scale-like filaments, bearing two to four anther cells, under the lower margin; fertile catkins, globular, of shield-shaped scales in four ranks, bearing several erect, bottle-shaped ovules; cone, globular, firmly closed, but opening at maturity; the scales thick and woody, pointed or bossed in the middle; the narrowly winged seeds attached to their contracted base or stalk; cotyledons, two or three.

Cupressus thyoides—White Cedar.

Leaves, very small, ovate with a small gland on the back, closely imbricated in four rows on the two-edged branchlets; anther cells, two under each scale.

The White Cedar is found in swamps near the sea coast from Massachusetts to Florida, but appears to be unknown in the interior, the tree bearing that name in western New York and Wisconsin being the Arbor Vitæ (Thuja occidentalis.) It rises with a straight trunk seventy or eighty feet, and when grown closely is destitute of branches for three-fourths of its height. The wood is light, easily worked, and exceedingly durable. It is preferred to any other for the manufacture of woodenware for household use; and shingles made from it are more highly valued than any other.

Whether or not this tree could be successfully grown for timber in other localities than its native swamps, is a question which I am unable to decide. It is rarely advertised in nursery catalogues, although it appears to have stronger claims to notice as an ornamental tree than many others cultivated for that purpose. According to Michaux its growth is slow.

Cupressus Lawsoniana (Lawson's Cypress), is a species of great beauty from California, where it grows to a large size, and affords valuable timber. The foliage is graceful and delicate, of feathery lightness, and bluish-green color; the ends of the branches are drooping. It is hardy around New York, and it is hoped may prove so in Illinois. Mr. Douglas raises it successfully from seed. The seedlings vary greatly in form, some being spreading, others quite fastigiate.

C. Nootkaensis (Nootka Sound Cypress), is from the Pacific coast, and is a tree of large size, much resembling the preceding when small—perhaps somewhat less beautiful, but more hardy. It has been propagated by nurserymen under the name of Thuiopsis borealis. In its native country it is said to grow from eighty to one hundred feet high.

JUNIPERUS—JUNIPER.

Flowers, diœcious, rarely monœcious; anther cells, three to six, attached to the lower edge of the scale; fertile catkins, ovoid, of three to six, fleshy, one to three, ovuled caulescent scales, becoming a sort of a berry, scaly bracted at the base; seeds, one to three, bony; cotyledons, two.

The Junipers are a numerous family, mostly of foreign origin. A few are of large size, and afford valuable timber; but the greater part are mere shrubs or dwarfish trees, fit only for amateur culture. The most valuable foreign species are unsuited to the climate of the Northern States, or are imperfectly tested. Three or four species are found within the limits of the United States.

Juniperus Virginiana—Red Cedar.

Leaves, four-ranked, very numerous; on old twigs very small and scale-like, closely imbricated; on thrifty shoots, awl-shaped and somewhat spreading, in pairs or threes.

The Red Cedar is known throughout the United States east of the Rocky Mountains, but is most common near the sea coast. According to Michaux, the further south and nearer the sea it grows, the better is its wood. Its ordinary height does not exceed thirty or forty feet, with a diameter of ten or twelve inches, which decreases rapidly. The wood is highly valued for its great durability; when it can be procured it is employed in ship building, and when used for posts, it will last forty or fifty years. It is much used in the manufacture of lead pencils. The tree varies greatly in form. Ordinarily it is more or less spreading, and the lower branches of a tree, ten feet high, are often as long as the trunk. Others are more conical, and along the Hudson river it grows in a form as fastigiate as that of the Lombardy Poplar.

Some writers have recommended the Red Cedar as the best tree for screens and shelter belts. As far as my experience qualifies me to judge, it is inferior for that purpose to almost any other evergreen in common cultivation. It is of slower growth than even the Arbor Vitæ and Hemlock; and when grown in the rich loam of the Western prairies it is sometimes completely killed even when ten or twelve feet high. As an ornamental hedge it is not desirable. After a few years it becomes thin at the base, and ragged and unsightly in appearance.

If sown when ripe the seed will seldom vegetate until the second year. The berries should be mixed with an equal quantity of sand, buried in the earth and allowed to remain one year. If then sown, most of it will germinate, although a part will sometimes not appear till the following year. The plants require protection from the sun when they first come up. Young plants are brought from Tennessee and other places in the South, but as far as my observation has extended, they are less hardy than those of Northern origin.

Where the Red Cedar springs up naturally, its growth should be encouraged; but other trees of equal value can be grown in artificial plantations with so much greater facility that there is little reason to anticipate its extensive culture for timber.

2. *Juniperus communis—Common Juniper.*

Leaves, in threes, linear, awl-shaped, prickly pointed, spreading, bright green except the glaucous-white upper surface.

The Common Juniper is a native both of America and the Eastern Continent, growing principally in northern latitudes. In America it is rarely if ever found in any other form than that of a prostrate straggling shrub, but some of the European varieties attain the size of a small tree. The berries are used for medicinal purposes, and are employed in flavoring gin. The Swedish and Irish Junipers, well known in ornamental cultivation, are varieties of this species. They are propagated principally by cuttings, rooted by means of bottom-heat. The young shoots of both are sometimes injured in severe winters, when they have not made a well ripened growth.

TAXODIUM.

Flowers, monœcious on the same branch; sterile catkins, spiked-panicled, of few stamens; filaments scale-like, bearing from two to five anther cells; fertile catkins, ovoid, clustered, scaly, with two ovules at the base of each scale; cones, globular, with angular, woody, thick shield-shaped scales; leaves, two-ranked, linear, deciduous; cotyledons, six to nine.

Taxodium distichum—Deciduous Cypress.

Leaflets, short, one-half to one inch long, linear, spreading, awl-shaped and imbricated on flowering branchlets; branchlets often drooping.

The Deciduous Cypress belongs more particularly to the Southern States, but is found within the limits assigned to this work. In Delaware, Maryland and Virginia it grows near the sea coast; and also in Kentucky, Southern Illinois and Missouri, near the Mississippi river. It formerly existed in considerable quantity near Cape Girardeau, in Missouri, but near its northern natural limit it does not reach the size to which it attains further south. In the vicinity of the Lower Mississippi it is often one hundred and twenty feet high, with a straight, clean shaft, destitute of branches for the greater part of its height, and a spreading flattened summit. It grows almost exclusively in swamps and alluvial lands. In the bayous, and ponds called alligator holes, in the bottom lands of the Yazoo and other southern rivers, the Cypress is often seen in company with the Tupelo, growing in water three or four feet deep, the trunks standing so thickly that there is not room to wield an axe among them. The water flowing from these ponds has the appearance of French brandy, a color said to be communicated to it by the roots of the Cypress trees.

With regard to the value of the wood, Michaux says: "It is fine-grained, and after being some time exposed to light, of a reddish color; it possesses great strength and elasticity, and is lighter and less resinous than that of the Pines. To these properties is added the faculty of long resisting the heat and moisture of the Southern climate."

The wood is employed for most purposes for which Pine is used, and is far more durable. Posts made from it last a long time in the ground. Cypress shingles last forty years. Sugar-hogsheads and casks for containing molasses are made of it. Trees which grow where they are surrounded by water a great part of the year, are called White Cypresses; those grown in dryer lands, Black Cypresses. The wood of the latter is heavier, more resinous and darker colored than that of the former.

In its native countries the Cypress is of inestimable value. Its cultivation for timber would doubtless succeed as far north as St. Louis, perhaps further. It thrives best in moist soils, or situations where the roots will have access to water. It endures the climate of Northern Illinois, but its growth is checked by the severity of the winters, the trees being sometimes split or otherwise injured by the intense cold. These circumstances preclude the idea of its successful culture as a timber tree in that latitude. Its light, graceful foliage and handsome appearance entitle it to notice for ornamental purposes wherever the climate is not too severe. It is more easily raised from seed than most other trees of its class. Michaux makes the following remarks in regard to its propagation:

"The Cypress is multiplied from seed, which is the best method; by layers and by slips. In the beginning of spring the seeds are sown and lightly covered in vessels filled with mould and sand. The young plants must be kept in the shade and protected from frost. To obtain good seed, in March or April select the cones which begin to open, and store them in a dry place; the seeds which fall out are best; those which are obtained by opening the cones rarely germinate."

The Cypress should be transplanted while small, as the roots descend deeply into the earth wherever the nature of the soil permits.

THUJA.

Flowers, monœcious, terminal on different branches; male catkins, elliptical or ovoid, each flower bearing four anther cells, attached to the inner side of the scale; female catkins, ovoid, of few imbricated scales, fixed by the base, each bearing two erect ovules.

Thuja occidentalis—American Arbor Vitæ.

Leaves, appressed, imbricated in four rows on the two-edged branchlets; scales of the cones, pointless; seeds, broadly winged, all round.

The Arbor Vitæ is common in the most northern States of the Union, and in the British Provinces; but is rare in more southern latitudes. It grows in swamps, which it frequently occupies almost exclusively—in rocky situations—on the banks of streams, and the borders of lakes. It is forty or fifty feet in height, with a diameter of from twelve to fifteen inches, though it is sometimes much larger. In the neighborhood of the lakes it is called White Cedar; but as it is generally known among cultivators by the name of Arbor Vitæ, I have preferred it, since the other belongs also to Cupressus thyoides.

The wood of the Arbor Vitæ is light, soft and very durable. Michaux says it will last thirty-five or forty years when used for posts. Rails made from it last sixty years. It is largely employed for fencing, and is preferred for telegraph poles. The trunk tapers rapidly; it is therefore not used where sticks of considerable length and uniform diameter are required.

The Arbor Vitæ is generally admitted to be one of the very best evergreens for ornamental hedges and screens. It bears pruning to any extent desired, and plants that have been rendered compact by clipping, retain the fresh green of their leaves in winter better than those with more open foliage. It is somewhat prone to send up two or more leaders, but only one should be permitted to grow if a symmetrical tree is desired. For an ornamental hedge or low screen, the plants may be set fifteen or eighteen inches apart in a single row. For a screen designed for protection, two or more rows should be planted six feet apart, in the rows, and so placed as to be opposite the spaces in the next row. When designed for timber they must be planted thickly like other trees. Although growing mostly in swamps, the Arbor Vitæ thrives upon the Western prairies; indeed, it will do so in most soils except stiff clays. It roots readily from layers and cuttings.

In propagation by seed, the Arbor Vitæ shows a considerable tendency to the production of varieties. In the grounds of Robert Douglas, of Waukegan, Illinois, I saw many plants which he had selected from his seed beds; some of which gave promise of becoming desirable acquisitions. Some of these had their leaves tipped with silvery white; others had the hue of the Golden Arbor Vitæ, while some appeared nearly identical with the Siberian. Dwarf varieties are sometimes found among plants brought from the forest. There are several named varieties in cultivation, of which only three will be noticed here.

Var. Siberica (Siberian Arbor Vitæ) is of much slower growth than the species; its form is more compact, and its foliage more dense. It retains the dark green hue of its foliage well during the winter, and is esteemed for ornamental hedges. There can be little doubt that it is, as Hoopes asserts, a variety of the American Arbor Vitæ. Plants closely resembling it occur not unfrequently among seedlings of that species. There is no reason to believe that it ever grew in the country whose name it bears.

Var. plicata (Nee's Arbor Vitæ) is a variety from the Pacific coast. It is quite distinct and handsome, with twisted branches; but is as yet much less common in cultivation than the preceding. It is quite hardy.

Var. ericoides (Heath-leaved Arbor Vitæ) was introduced from Europe not many years since. It is a pretty shrub, with heath-like leaves of a dark-bluish green color, but often becoming brown in winter.

Thuja gigantea (Gigantic Arbor Vitæ) is a species of immense size from Oregon. It has not generally succeeded well in the Northern or Middle States.

Biota orientalis (Chinese Arbor Vitæ). I have found the cultivation of this and its most hardy varieties wholly unsatisfactory in Northern Illinois. Where it succeeds it is far inferior to the American species for ornament, and is of no value for any other purpose.

Retinospora obtusa (Japanese Arbor Vitæ) is a beautiful tree, somewhat resembling the American Arbor Vitæ, but with more delicate and graceful foliage. For several years it has withstood the winters of Northern Illinois in a partially sheltered situation, and it is hoped it may prove entirely hardy. Gray places it among the Cypresses (*Cupressus pisifera, var. obtusa*).

Sub Order, Taxineæ.

SALISBURIA.

Staminate flowers, axillary, filiform, pedunculate; fertile flowers, terminal, solitary, on simple or branching peduncles; ovule, in a cup-shaped disk, the disk becoming fleshy, embracing the base of the nut-like seed.

Salisburia adiantifolia—Ginko.

Leaves, pectinate, somewhat wedge-shaped at the base, irregularly cut on the margin, and marked with straight, divergent veins.

The Ginko has its origin in Japan, and in its native country is said to grow to a very large size. It is cultivated in America as an ornamental tree, and is admired for the singularity of its foliage. It is nearly quite hardy in Northern Illinois, the leading shoot only being occasionally somewhat injured by severe winters, after a season of ill-matured growth. The quality of its wood does not appear to be well ascertained. It is commonly propagated by layers or cuttings, although plants grown from seed are said to become the finest trees. As yet there are few trees producing seed in America. The tree is diœcious.

TAXUS—YEW.

Flowers, mostly diœcious, axillary; sterile catkins, small, globular, few flowered; anther cells, three to eight, under a shield-like scale; fertile flowers, solitary, scaly, bracted, consisting of an erect sessile ovule in the cup-shaped disk, which becomes pulpy and berry-like in fruit, nearly enclosing the nut-like seed; cotyledons, two.

Taxus baccata—English Yew.

Leaves, two-ranked, crowded, linear, flat; receptacle of the barren flowers, globular.

The Yew is a native of Europe and Asia. It is of very slow growth, and becomes in time a very large but not a very lofty tree. It is extremely long-lived; there are trees in England which are believed to be more than one thousand years old. From time immemorial it has been planted in church yards, probably on account of its dark-colored foliage. The wood combines all the most valuable qualities, being strong, heavy, fine grained, very elastic, and unexcelled in durability.

Although the Yew grows in Europe as far north as latitude 58,° it is not suited to the climate of the northern part of the United States. According to Hoopes, its culture near Philadelphia is unsatisfactory and its duration uncertain. If planted it should be in a shaded situation where it will not be exposed to the direct rays of the sun.

Var. Canadensis—American Yew, Ground Hemlock.

This was formerly described as a different species. It grows in the Northern States and in Canada,

American Arbor Vitæ.

almost always in evergreen woods. It is found in some localities in Illinois among rocks, in company with the Red Cedar, where it is uniformly a prostrate straggling shrub. I have seen it in cold, dark evergreen forests in New England; the prostrate stem extending ten or fifteen feet, buried and rooted in the leaves and mould, and throwing up, at intervals of one or two feet, nearly upright branches from two to four or even five feet in height. From this mode of growth it is often called Running Hemlock. In such situations it retains the dark green of its foliage unchanged through the winter. This variety is perfectly hardy, and attains a greater size in cultivation than when growing wild. Like the English Yew, it may be pruned into almost any form. Except when it is thickly shaded, the foliage becomes rusty or dingy during the winter.

There are a number of varieties of European origin, but they are little if at all more hardy than the English Yew. Other species exist which are not generally known, or as yet well tested.

CHAPTER XVII.

BROAD-LEAVED EVERGREENS, NOT CONIFEROUS.

Very few of this class of evergreens succeed in the northern part of the United States; probably none near their boundary. There are nevertheless some which are hardy in a large portion of the territory for which this work is designed; and, though none of them are of great value for timber culture, and some hardly entitled to the appellation of trees, I have thought proper to describe them.

BUXUS—BOX.

Natural Order, Euphorbiaceæ.

Calyx of the male flower, three-leaved; petals, two; stamens, four, inserted under the rudiment of a pistil; female calyx, four-leaved, with three petals and three styles; capsules, with three beaks; cells, three.

Buxus sempervirens—Boxtree.

Disk of the leaf, ovate, convex; footstalk, slightly downy at the edges; anthers, ovate, arrow-shaped.

The Box is a native of the temperate climates of Europe and Asia, growing to the height of from fifteen to thirty feet. Still larger trees are said to exist near Philadelphia. The wood is yellow, very hard and fine grained, and so heavy as to sink in water. It is used in the manufacture of mathematical and musical instruments, but principally for wood engraving. In gardens the tree was formerly much employed in what was called topiary work, and cut into the forms of men, and animals, and all kinds of geometrical and fanciful figures.

The Box is a beautiful tree, and appears to great advantage in winter, particularly when the ground is covered with snow. Its foliage is most brilliant when partially shaded by other trees. It has generally been regarded as too tender for the climate of northern Illinois. Mr. Douglas, of Waukegan, nevertheless cultivates it successfully without any other protection than what is afforded by belts of trees; a fact which should encourage others to attempt its culture. It is propagated by seeds, layers or cuttings. The seeds should be sown as soon as ripe in dry rich mould in a shaded situation. It is more commonly grown from cuttings from four to six inches long, which readily root if put early in the fall in a frame of sandy soil. The Box transplants well with ordinary care.

Var. suffruticosa (Dwarf Box) is employed for edging garden walks. It will not endure the winters of northern Illinois without protection. covering of snow is sufficient, but it must be kept on all winter. If other means are used, care must be taken not to cover so close as to smother the plants.

ILEX—HOLLY.

Natural Order, Aquifoliaceae.

Flowers, more or less diœciously polygamous, but many of them perfect; calyx, four to six-toothed; petals, four to six, separate or united only at the base; stamens, four to six; berry, four to eight seeded; leaves, alternate.

Ilex opaca—American Holly.

Leaves, oval, flat, spiny, the margins wavy; flowers in clusters at the base of the young branches and in the axils; calyx teeth acute.

The American Holly is found near the Atlantic coast from Maine to Florida. On the Mississippi and its tributaries it grows as far north as West Tennessee. It is found in Arkansas and the Indian territory. In these countries it attains its fullest development in rich bottom lands. I have seen it in Northern Mississippi from forty to sixty feet in height. On the coast of New England it is a shrub or small tree. It thrives best in deep rich loam; it will grow in dry sandy soil, but not in cold, wet lands or stiff clays.

The wood of the Holly is white, heavy, hard, and fine grained. It is esteemed for turning, and is applied to many uses for which the Box is valued. The tree is nowhere abundant, and is of slow growth.

It is, therefore, esteemed principally for ornamental purposes. Few trees are as beautiful as the Holly, particularly in the season when deciduous trees are destitute of leaves. Very beautiful ornamental hedges may be made of it. Wherever it can be successfully grown, it merits far more attention than has as yet been bestowed upon it.

It is not yet satisfactorily determined how far north in the Mississippi Valley the Holly will succeed. The only attempt at its culture I have ever known in Illinois was an unsucessful one, by C. R. Overman, of Bloomington. In this case the plants were brought from far south; I think from Texas; it can, therefore, hardly be considered a fair test. Where the winters are too cold, the leaves brown badly, and are sometimes entirely destroyed.

The Holly is propagated by seeds and cuttings. The berries when ripe are mixed with sand, put in a box, and buried where they will keep moist. A year from the following spring they are taken up and sown in beds. The seeds should be thinly covered, and the surface kept moist by a light covering of rotten leaves or moss. While in the nursery the young plants should be transplanted every two years to keep the roots in proper condition for their final removal.

I. aquifolium (European Holly) is a beautiful tree, but not hardy as far north as Philadelphia. It is treated in the same manner as the American species. Other evergreen Hollies are found in the Southern States, but none of them are hardy at the North.

KALMIA.

Natural Order, Ericaceæ.

Calyx, five-parted; corolla, between wheel-shaped and bell-shaped, five-lobed, with ten depressions, in which the ten anthers are severally lodged until they begin to shed their pollen; filaments, thread form; pod, globose, five-celled, many-seeded.

1. *Kalmia latifolia—Laurel, Mountain Laurel.*

Leaves, mostly alternate, bright green both sides, ovate-lanceolate or elliptical, tapering to each end, petioled; corymbs, terminal, many-flowered, clammy, pubescent; pod, depressed, glandular.

The Mountain Laurel is common in many parts of Massachusetts, and is said to be found in some localities still further north. It is abundant southward along the Alleghany Mountains. It often forms dense thickets; which the crooked and unyielding stems interlocked with each other, render almost impenetrable. It is commonly a shrub from six to ten feet high, but in favorable situations becomes a small tree. According to Torrey it is found twenty feet high on the Catskill Mountains, and it is said to exceed this size in the Southern States. I well remember the former existence of specimens near my native place, in localities as yet undisturbed by the wood-chopper, which were fifteen feet high and three inches in diameter; but they have long since disappeared.

The wood of the Laurel more nearly resembles Boxwood than that of any other American tree; and is well fitted to supply its place. It is very hard and close grained, and takes a fine polish. It was formerly used by the Indians and backwoods settlers for making wooden spoons, and was often called Spoonwood.

No one who has ever seen the Laurel in bloom needs to be reminded of its beauty. The flowers are always numerous, varying from pure white to a beautiful rose color. They are arranged in corymbs at the ends of the branches, and their brilliant effect is increased by the richness of the surrounding foliage. The bloom continues several weeks.

The Laurel withstands the winters of Northern Illinois perfectly well; but care is necessary to provide it with a suitable soil. It is said not to live long in limestone clays. I have found it to thrive in the black mould of the prairies, particularly if mixed with swamp muck and rotten chips. A cool northern exposure, or shaded situation, suits it best; in such places its foliage is more brilliant, and fresher than if exposed to the full rays of the sun.

Plants of considerable size, transplanted from their native localities, seldom survive. Those growing in open ground are to be preferred, and if small, well-rooted plants are selected, they will generally succeed. The seed is minute and the skill of a gardener is required to raise plants from it. Michaux remarks that many years are necessary to obtain plants from the seed in a condition to bloom. This may be the case, but I have received plants which did not appear to be very old, that began to flower when less than a foot high.

2. *Kalmia angustifolia—Sheep Laurel.*

Leaves, commonly opposite or in threes, pale or whitish underneath, light green above, narrowly oblong, obtuse, petioled; corymbs, lateral, slightly glanular, many flowered.

The Sheep Laurel is common in many parts of the Atlantic States, growing to the height of two or three feet, in clumps or beds. The flowers are similar to those of the preceding species, but are only one-third the size, and are of a deeper red. It is very ornamental, and continues a long time in bloom.

This species has the reputation of being poisonous to sheep, and is somtimes called Lambkill. Sheep, however, will eat it only in the winter, when other green forage is not to be had. It is probable that the mischief is occasioned by the indigestible nature of the leaves rather than by any poisonous property which they possess.

Two other species, K. glauca and K. hirsuta, are found in swamps, but they are quite small and rarely, if ever, cultivated.

RHODODENDRON—ROSE BAY.

Natural Order, Ericaceæ.

Calyx, five-parted; corolla, bell-shaped, or partly funnel-form, five-lobed; stamens, ten, declined; anthers, opening by two terminal pores; pods, five-celled, five-valved, many-seeded.

1. *Rhododendron maximum—Great Laurel.*

Leaves, elliptical, oblong or lance-oblong, acute, narrowed towards the base, very smooth, with somewhat revolute margins; corolla, bell-shaped.

This species is found in New England, but much more abundantly further south. Cool, moist, deeply-shaded situations seem most congenial to its nature. It abounds on the banks of torrents among the Alleghany Mountains, and grows in the miry soil of Cedar swamps. It is a plant of great beauty, both of flowers and foliage. It is most commonly a shrub not more than ten feet high, but sometimes reaches twenty or twenty-five feet. The flowers are usually rose-colored with yellow dots inside, but are sometimes pure white. The leaves are very thick and smooth, and are from four to ten inches long.

Although a native of several of the Northern States, this species appears to be much less common in cultivation than the R. Catawbiense. This is probably owing to its greater shyness of cultivation in gardens, where it is not always practicable to give it the moist atmosphere and shade which seem to be indispensable.

2. *Rhododendron Catawbiense—Rose bay.*

Leaves, oval or oblong, rounded at both ends, smooth, pale beneath, three to five inches long; corolla, broadly bell-shaped, lilac purple; pedicels, rusty, downy.

The high summits of the Alleghanies, from Virginia southward, are the native home of this species.

It is smaller than the preceding, seldom becoming more than six feet high. It is one of the most beautiful shrubs in cultivation. Many hybrids have been produced between this and R. Ponticum, a less hardy species from Asia. It is said to be hardy throughout the United States, but, like some others of the same natural order, it will not grow in soils impregnated with lime. Where such exists, it is necessary to prepare a bed largely composed of swamp muck and rotten wood for the reception of the plants.

CHAPTER XVIII.

LIST OF MOST VALUABLE TIMBER TREES.

The following is a list of the most valuable timber trees for cultivation in the section of the United States to which this work is limited, viz.: for the northern portion of the United States, from the Atlantic ocean westward to the Rocky Mountains, and extending southward to include Virginia, Kentucky, Missouri and Kansas, as stated in Preface

1. White Oak—Quercus alba.
2. Bur Oak—Q. macrocarpa.
3. Sugar Maple—Acer saccharinum.
4. White Ash—Fraxinus Americana.
5. Blue Ash—F. quadrangulata.
6. Red Ash—F. pubescens.
7. Black Walnut—Juglans nigra.
8. Butternut—J. cinerea.
9. Chestnut—Castanea vesca.
10. Shellbark Hickory—Carya alba.
11. Pignut Hickory—C. glabra.
12. Linden, or Basswood—Tilia Americana.
13. Tulip Tree—Liriodendron tulipifera.

14. European Larch—Larix Europea.
15. Norway Spruce—Abies excelsa.
16. White Pine—Pinus strobus.
17. Scotch Pine—P. sylvestris.
18. Red Pine—P. resinosa.
19. Corsican Pine—P. Laricio.
20. Catalpa—Catalpa bignonioides.

Of this list, Nos. 5, 6, 13, 19 and 20 are best suited to the climate of the southern half of the territory for which this work is designed. No. 7 and No. 9 would, probably, not succeed in the most northern part of the United States; while Nos. 4, 12, 16, 17 and 18 would be of doubtful value near the southern limit.

Balsam Fir.

GENERAL INDEX.

INDEX OF SCIENTIFIC NAMES.

Those in italics are noticed without particular description.

INDEX OF COMMON NAMES.

www.ingramcontent.com/pod-product-compliance
Lightning Source LLC
LaVergne TN
LVHW010231110826
845151LV00004B/1255

* 9 7 8 1 4 2 5 5 2 5 7 8 1 *